Anyone who has had the privilege of learning from Coach Dar knows she offers sage counsel and guidance, and as a person she is truly one of a kind. When applying her leadership principles, our executive team was able to successfully lead a Fortune 500 Company through the uncharted waters of a global pandemic and come out on the other side stronger and more aligned than ever.

—**Sheryl Palmer,** Chairman and CEO of
Taylor Morrison

Coach Dar is an amazing person and catalyst for true change when it comes to personal life or leadership of businesses in need of bouncing back. I have worked with her for more than 10 years and greatly benefitted from her skills and advice.

—**Erik Olsson,** Board Chairman of Willscot
Mobile Mini, Inc. and Ritchie Bros. and Board
Member of Pontem Corp. and Domestic Group

You may already know that I am a big fan of Coach Dar's work. In *The Art of Bouncing Back*, she leads you through the exact steps that she uses with professional athletes and executives to help them overcome life's challenges. Read this book yourself and then pay it forward to a friend who needs to bounce back and find their flow again.

—**Thaddeus Bullard,** also known as Titus O'Neil
and WWE Global Ambassador

The Art of Bouncing Back is a must-read! Having come back from several strokes in her twenties to become the renowned performance coach she is now is truly incredible. She is the personification of the word *resilience*! The book is authoritative and encouraging. There is something in it for everyone.

—**John H. Dalton,** 70th Secretary of the Navy

THE ART OF
BOUNCING BACK

Here's to

THE ART OF
BOUNCING BACK

FIND YOUR FLOW TO

THRIVE AT WORK AND IN LIFE

ANY TIME YOU'RE OFF YOUR GAME

DARLEEN SANTORE

KNOWN AS

"COACH DAR"

Mc
Graw
Hill

New York Chicago San Francisco Athens London Madrid
Mexico City Milan New Delhi Singapore Sydney Toronto

1 2 3 4 5 6 7 8 9   LCR   28 27 26 25 24 23

ISBN   978-1-264-85402-8
MHID   1-264-85402-1

e-ISBN   978-1-264-85490-5
e-MHID   1-264-85490-0

McGraw Hill books are available at special quantity discounts to use as premiums and sales promotions or for use in corporate training programs. To contact a representative, please visit the Contact Us pages at www.mhprofessional.com.

McGraw Hill is committed to making our products accessible to all learners. To learn more about the available support and accommodations we offer, please contact us at accessibility@mheducation.com. We also participate in the Access Text Network (www.accesstext.org), and ATN members may submit requests through ATN.

To my mom.

As a child, I'd spend the summers going to my
mom's beauty shop. She would take me to this little
independent bookstore nearby (RJ Julia Booksellers
in Madison, Connecticut) to pick out something
to read while I waited for her to be finished with
work. She would point to the shelves and say,
"One day your book's going to be in here."

In 2012, when I first shared with her the news that
I was finally going to make that dream a reality,
no one was more excited for me than she was.
While my mom has since passed, I have felt her
encouragement throughout this entire writing process.

Mom, you were the true embodiment of bouncing
back. Your resilience, grit, sense of purpose, and
ability to move forward still inspire me to this day.

Linny, this is for you!

CONTENTS

FOREWORD

Almost five years ago I had received a message from this woman who was the leadership and mental skills coach for the Phoenix Suns. She shared how a few of my books had made such an impact on her and the athletes she worked with that she wanted to order more for the locker room. This led to me learning more about this woman known to many as Coach Dar. After learning more, I quickly asked her to share her story and be a speaker on my virtual Power of Positive Summit.

A month after that she and I were sharing the stage together as keynote speakers at a sports and faith conference.

It was then that I got to truly experience what many have come to know as "a dose of Dar." Her faith, energy, and passion for what she does exuded throughout the conference room. This pint-size powerhouse had much to share.

What stood out to me was that she was giving this speech just weeks after having a stroke. If that is not a great example of resilience and bouncing back, I don't know what is. When she went up to speak, she shared that sometimes her words don't come out correctly and that she might have to sit because she loses her balance due to the stroke.

In true Dar form, she pressed on and did great.

It is no mistake that she has now written a book, *The Art of Bouncing Back*, because her life, as you will read, is an exceptional example on how to do just that: bounce back. And after 26 years helping thousands of people bounce back from all kinds of adversity, she is sharing for the first time her exact game plan and principles on how to do just that. This book is filled with the exact techniques she uses with professional athletes and CEOs around the world. And now you get to have access to them, too.

Her character and resilience are unmatched, and her love for people and passion to help everyone bounce back from adversity has led to this amazing and life-changing book. I'm so thankful she wrote it and am fired up you are reading it.

It has been a blessing getting to know Coach Dar both as her mentor and friend and know you will enjoy learning from her as well.

Life gets hard, we can't escape that, but we can learn how to bounce back from it all.

—Jon Gordon
Bestselling author and keynote speaker.
Author of 26 books including multiple bestsellers:
The Energy Bus, The Carpenter, Training Camp, You Win the Locker Room First, and *The Power of Positive Leadership.*

INTRODUCTION

I like to say that setbacks don't define you,
and comebacks only refine you.

—Dar

O n the cover of this book is a bouncy ball. You have
no idea how much time and consideration were put
into that bouncy ball. It really is the best illustra-
tion of how adversity can show up in our life and create more
potential than problems. If you've ever played with a bouncy
ball, you know that the harder you throw it against a surface,
the higher the ball bounces back. It's the same with life. The
"harder" our adversities are, the "higher" we can bounce back.

I specialize in helping some of the best of the best get up
and move forward from some of life's most challenging situations, including:

- Losing their position to a new player to finding a
  leadership position on the team
- Floundering professionally to then getting a C-suite
  position

- Being a leader who's been thrown off their game to regaining confidence and building more influence than ever
- Running a foundation with massive cracks to rebuilding on solid footing
- Experiencing financial devastation to regaining miles of margin
- Being in a slump in sports to coming back and being named an all-star
- Facing a season-ending injury to coming back better than before, both on and off the court as a player, parent, and human

These are all true stories from my career working with some of the most elite athletes and accomplished CEOs in the world.

They call me Coach Dar. Put simply, my job is to help people stay mentally sharp and get people back into the game of life after a gut punch (or several) has put them on the sidelines. I combine science, psychology, leadership, and three decades of professional wisdom to change the way they respond to challenges, obstacles, and mental blocks. I have worked with accomplished CEOs who have suffered massive business losses, divorcees, folks starting again personally and professionally, entrepreneurs catching their breath after a major setback, pro athletes in the top 1 percent of their game, and groups (faith-based and beyond) that have one more chance to pull it together.

I've also coached leaders across the globe—at Kennedys, Comcast, the San Diego Padres, the Phoenix Suns, the Indiana Pacers, Indiana Fever, Charter Spectrum, Taylor

Morrison, Big Machine Records, Rodan + Fields, Sunrider, Jon Gordon Power of Positive Summit, Powerhouse Women, Integrating Women Leaders, Origami Owl, YMCA, Mobile Mini Solutions, PathNorth, Vail Resorts, and Georgetown University, as well as players within the Women's National Basketball Association (WNBA), Major League Baseball (MLB), the National Football League (NFL), the National Basketball Association (NBA), the National Hockey League (NHL), and many more. They all understand the extreme value in helping their organizations learn how to bounce back faster from disruptions.

I share all of this with you because I know you need to trust me if you're going to take the coaching I'm offering and put it into practice.

This book lays out the system I've used to help all of these incredible human beings. It's called the Bounce Back Coaching System, and together we'll work through the nine specific principles of this system so you can bounce back from anything. Because this is something I need you to know: *no matter what's going on in your life right now, no matter who is at fault, who is to blame, you really can bounce back from anything.*

THE NINE PRINCIPLES OF THE BOUNCE BACK COACHING SYSTEM

My Bounce Back Coaching System takes you through nine principles, each of which delivers specific strategies and techniques that allow you to turn setbacks into setups.

They include:

Principle 1: Embracing the Suck

Principle 2: Understanding Who You Are

Principle 3: Seeking and Applying Feedback

Principle 4: Discovering Your Why Power

Principle 5: Creating Your Bounce Back Environment

Principle 6: Activating Emotional Intelligence

Principle 7: Reframing Setbacks

Principle 8: Cultivating Grit

Principle 9: Turning the Page

Each principle will deliver proven and science-backed tools to help you respond to challenges, obstacles, and mental blocks in helpful and productive ways. Through exercises in each chapter, you'll experience self-discovery and the deep work needed to make it through and come out better in your current and future setbacks. If you've done similar exercises already, I want you to push those to the side and start over. Do a reset. Some of the most important mental work you'll ever do is the deconstruction of long-held beliefs and principles that no longer serve you—or maybe some that never served you at all.

In Principles 1 through 6, you'll learn how to pour your emotional foundation. Get ready to embrace the suck, get a deep understanding of your Fundamental Hardwiring, know everything you need to know about feedback (including why it's so important to growth and bouncing back), connect with your Why Power, create your own Bounce Back Environment, and activate your Emotional Intelligence. Through each of these principles, you'll learn so much about yourself and will be able to identify the exact pivot that needs to happen to push forward and make you mentally tougher so you can handle future adversity better.

In Principles 7 and 8, you'll apply your knowledge of previous principles so you can start reframing your setbacks and cultivating the grit needed to bounce back even better from each one.

And, finally, in Principle 9, you'll learn how to "turn the page" even in the toughest of situations and relationships. And, you'll be fully equipped with the tools, motivation, and inspiration you need to start again. This is where you go from just surviving to thriving again, from pain to purpose, from struggle to strength, and from adversity to advancement.

Additional resources, videos, and tools to support your reading journey are available at coachdar.com/new-book.

Through these nine principles, not only will we build a rock-solid foundation, we will also break down how you operate day-to-day to reveal how and where you're really showing up (or not showing up). We'll focus on the accountability, growth mindset, thought-habits, and positive patterns that will help and enable you to reframe the way you view obstacles going forward. You'll start to see them as opportunities—giving you the ability to move from pain to purpose in any situation.

We'll also work on your mental game. Whether you're coming to this book to grow personally or to help your employees or teammates do the same, I want you to think about building a house. Any stable home requires first pouring a solid foundation. It can't be a foundation that's slapped together hastily, and it can't be a foundation based on the measurements of someone else's house. The foundation of your home is your mental game, and the practices throughout this book are necessary to build your strong foundation. I know you're busy and you may think you can skip over some of the more abstract practices or exercises, but if you skip over them, you aren't pouring yourself the most secure stable foundation. You will remain stuck—your "house" falling further into the ground. So do the work. You'll come out better on the other side because of it.

WHAT YOU GET FROM APPLYING THESE PRINCIPLES

The results you will see after reading this book and applying the nine principles to your life will help you immensely when you put them into practice. I know that because I've seen incredible results of this work time and time again. Three of the most game-changing results happen to be flow, resilience, and raising the bar (a mental elevation of thinking and standards). I will talk to each of these throughout this book, which is why I feel it's critical that you understand exactly what I mean when I use each term. So let's define each now.

Flow

Flow happens when you are completely and fully present in the task at hand. You lose track of time. Every movement is fluid, your mind is clear, and your thoughts are on standby. You are at one with your body and mind—there is no separation or compartmentalization. It happens when you're clear on your vision, committed to raising the bar every day, and using your gifts, talents, and skills to align with your purpose. Flow is how you do your best work and achieve greatness.

Resilience

Think of resilience as your elasticity capacity—your ability to stretch yourself further mentally and emotionally when overcoming challenges. Resilience is necessary to recover quickly from difficulties and as you build up your resilience, you become more adept at bouncing back from tough situations.

Raising the Bar

Every one of my clients will tell you that they always hear me say "raise the bar" during a coaching session. Raising the bar is synonymous with achieving greatness. It's more than just another sports or business cliché, it's a mental elevation that creates big results. When you mentally raise the bar, you increase the standard for yourself daily. You push yourself to do what you do well and make the most with every set of 24 hours you're given.

• • •

As a result of the work you will do in the next 180-plus pages, flow, resilience, and mental elevation, aka raising the bar, will become accessible to you in even the toughest of situations. You'll be able to bounce back from adversity and move forward thanks to each and every skill you add to your mental skills toolbox.

You'll also be prepared to take massive action so you can outlast and outperform the version of you yesterday and dominate your life and the space you operate in. All thanks to the hard work you put into making that your new reality.

I want the nine principles in this book to help you be able to recover quickly from setbacks and plateaus so you can live a life with more flow. I want you to be resilient in the face of adversity. I want you to be able to achieve greatness by mentally raising the bar for yourself and those around you. And based on experience, I know all of that can happen for you.

If you can learn the art of bouncing back when the gut punches of life hit, they won't hit as hard and you won't stay down as long. So let's get to it.

EMBRACING THE SUCK

A setback often moves us to a road that is even
worse, but leads to an even better destination.
–Mokokoma Mokhonoana,
author of *The Confessions of a Misfit*

Have you ever noticed that when life punches you in the gut, you can lose your sense of humor and definitely your sense of purpose?

When I wake up every morning, I have two thoughts in this order: "Dar, you get to go awaken greatness in yourself and others as far and as wide as God allows today, so go live your mission," and then, "Be grateful for today because any day can be your last—or the day you have *your fourth stroke, so say the important things today.*"

You read that right. *Fourth stroke.* Up until this point, you may have pinned me as an ultrapositive and enthusiastic mental toughness coach and occupational therapist

9

who is always moving forward with the spirited delivery of an NFL football coach. While that's not wrong . . . it's not the whole truth either. The truth is I've had more than one major setback in my life that almost kept me from bouncing back, much less moving forward. I have been forced to practice what I preach. I say "forced" as there were several times when I was not able to listen to my own best advice because the gut punches took everything out of me.

Setback 1: I had my first stroke.

Setback 2: I was told I couldn't have kids.

Setback 3: I went through a divorce.

Setback 4: I had my second stroke.

Setback 5: I had a third stroke, which took away my ability to speak fluently.

Setback 6: My insurance wouldn't cover my rehabilitation.

Setback 7: I had no speaking gigs to help pay for my big medical bills.

Setback 8: My mother died.

Setback 9: My father died

Setbacks suck. They can feel like you are tumbling down a staircase with no landing at the bottom. The bottom seems elusive as you keep hitting one setback after another.

When you list out your setbacks like this, they stretch out like mile markers along the road of life. Of course, this isn't an exhaustive list—Lord knows there have been many more. Just like you, my life is marred with painful experiences.

People say, "Dar, how did you bounce back from all that?" And my answer is always the same: "What is the alternative?" Even after her own stroke and 11 surgeries, my mom would tell us: *If we are still alive, then we still have a chance and a reason to be here.* I truly believe that—for me and for you. (See Figure 1.1.)

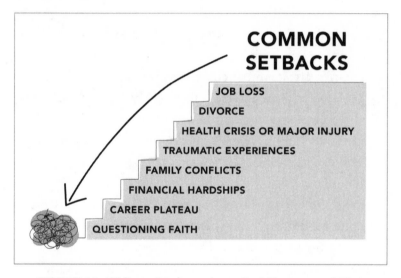

FIGURE 1.1. While setbacks make us feel like we are falling down stairs, often with no last step in sight, they don't have to feel that way. A setback is an interruption in progress, not a permanent landing. Building up your mental bounce back skills will help you feel more in control during tumultuous times.

There are two things that make it possible for me to bounce back and move forward: knowing my Why and controlling my environment, both of which we will fully explore in the next two chapters. In this chapter, we will focus on embracing the suck.

I'll say it again, setbacks suck.

SETBACKS HAPPEN WHEN YOU LEAST EXPECT THEM

I woke up in a hospital bed—*again*.

It wasn't my first rodeo—I'd already suffered two strokes prior to this. The hospital bed, the machines beeping, the flurry of activity, all too familiar. In a strange way, I woke up this third time with a sense of calm.

But before I tell you how this story ends, let me start over—at the beginning.

My first stroke didn't come with this same calm.

I've always been active. I played field hockey, ran track, lifted weights with my dad in our basement starting in the eighth grade, and have continued working out regularly my entire life.

Knowing this, when I hurt my back lifting a patient, I decided to go to the chiropractor to get an adjustment. I'd done all kinds of sciatica treatment up until that point, and nothing had worked. This was my last-ditch effort. I stopped in for a visit, got adjusted, and moved on to the next task. Over the next couple of days, I started experiencing moments of dizziness and blurred vision. I felt *off,* blaming it on working too much and being tired.

Then about a week later, I was working on a Saturday, walking down the hallway toward the stairs. All of a sudden, my world flipped upside down; the floor was the ceiling and the ceiling was the floor. My vision was wonky and I knew something had to be going on with my head. It was like my body had forgotten how to walk. I was frozen. My vision stayed inverted as I felt for the wall beside me. My muscle memory must have kicked in then, because my legs started moving me down the hallway to the staircase, where I walked down. Then it was like a light turned on in the dark and I could see again.

I upgraded my self-diagnosis from exhaustion to a sinus infection. *I'm just sick*, I convinced myself. *I've got compacted sinuses or something.* Meanwhile I was working in the stroke unit, so I should have been thinking differently. When I got to my office area, I called my dad.

"Dad, my vision's been weird. Can you pick me up from work? I don't think I should drive."

To this day, my dad says one of his biggest regrets in life is that he didn't drive me straight to the emergency room after I told him what happened. Over the next few days, my symptoms would come and go. I started taking Sudafed and felt groggy all the time. One night I started vomiting for no apparent reason, and my suspicions grew that there was something going on, something more than a sinus infection.

The following morning, I couldn't get my bearings. I started to get what we call "neural nystagmus," which is where your eyes start to shake uncontrollably for spells at a time. The truth was that my denial of what was really happening became painfully self-evident: *something is wrong—neurologically wrong.* I yelled for my husband and told him I needed help. "Get me a bowl to throw up in." I couldn't even make it out of the bed to the trash can or toilet.

Poor guy, he was so nervous seeing me—his strong, capable wife—in so much agony, that he brought me a colander. You know, one of those bowls with holes in them that you can drain water from pasta. Even in the middle of this, we laughed.

He loaded me up in the car and headed toward the hospital. I started going over the checklist in my head—the one I used with my stroke patients.

"There's three things you've got to tell them," I advised. "The first is this is *not* the flu. The second, since I'm staggering around and throwing up, is that I'm *not* drunk. And the last—don't let them send me home. Something is wrong."

Sure enough, they tried to say it was the flu, accused me of being drunk, and tried to send me home. After basically forcing myself into being seen for further tests, I was misdiagnosed with a tumor growing behind my ear. They thought this "tumor" was cutting off the blood supply to my brain and causing my symptoms. The next misdiagnosis I got was encephalitis—an infection in the tissue of the brain.

I'm a take-charge personality, so once I got the impression that no one *really* knew what was going on, I went out on my own and found a private neurologist to evaluate me. He said, "Dar, think. What happened? Did you get in an accident? Did you fall? There must have been some sort of trauma."

I was like, "Look, Doc. If I fell and hit my head, I think I'd remember that."

Thankfully, he was relentless and had me retrace my steps. Almost as an afterthought, I offered, "Well, I got adjusted at the chiropractor."

Immediately, he stood up. "Dar, we've got to get you into another MRI right now. I think they ripped an artery in your brain." I watched everyone's faces as they read my MRI. I knew he'd been right.

"The bad news," the doctor said, "is that you have a blood clot in your brain. It could dislodge any day. But there is some good news—scar tissue could form around the clot that could hold it in place."

"What happens if the blood clot moves out of place?" I asked.

"You could die."

OK, I thought. Not that this news wasn't alarming—it was. I just wasn't mentally capable of fully absorbing it at that moment. Situational numbness began to set in. The processing of this news would take years for me to fully understand my emotions. "Anything else I should know?"

"Yes. Don't run anymore . . .

Don't cough too hard . . .

Don't do anything that could raise your blood pressure . . .

Don't strain or push too hard especially when exercising . . ."

It felt like I was falling down stairs with every *don't.*

"Doc," I said, "that's a lot of don'ts. You're basically telling me not to live."

"Dar, you can live but you don't have the luxury of being careless with your body. And, you can't carry or deliver a child as the strain could kill you."

Don't.

Don't.

Don't.

Don't.

Don't have a baby?

That morning I had placed the book *What to Expect When You're Expecting* on my bedroom night table. I'm Italian, and my family had made it well-known that it was high time my husband and I started trying for a family. I was working as an occupational therapist at the time and very successfully specializing in helping patients recover from traumatic brain injuries. Rick and I had just bought our first home together. We had a five-year plan. Life was good.

I walked out of the doctor's office at 25 years of age with a diagnosis that made me feel 85. "My life was over before it had begun" was the singular thought plaguing my brain.

SETBACKS ALWAYS HAVE INCONVENIENT TIMING

I was 38 years old when I had my second stroke; this one was more so a warning sign to slow down (which I didn't right away).

Perhaps what was most unsettling was that I had felt like I was hitting my stride in life. By this point I had finally dealt with the pain of not being able to have children, gone through a divorce, accepted that I would not have what I thought was a traditional Italian American family dream, and both reset and found work I truly loved. I was leading, speaking, coaching, and empowering people. I was going full steam ahead (again), but the pace was too much and my body said "enough." The way it started was I went to throw out something with my right hand and my left hand released what was in it. I looked at my friend Tyson and said "That was weird."

Then the next morning I went to put concealer under my eyes and put it on my lips. The final indication that I needed to see my neurologist came when I went home to take a break by the beach. I was playing Yahtzee with my sister, and she handed the dice to me while she took a sip of water. I then took the Yahtzee cup with the dice in them and instead of rolling the dice, I lifted the cup to sip out of it. My sister said, "What are you doing?" I knew then I was freakin' having another stroke.

I went in to see my neurologist and sure enough he said, "Darleen, you are having another stroke." While it was more mild than before, I had what they call motor apraxia, which is when you know what you want to do with an item, but you do something else with it. Meaning, you know, you take the toothbrush to your teeth, but you end up trying to brush your hair with it. It's so weird. This went on for a while, but I know how to manage and rehab it now as it was something I was trained in to help my stroke patients as an occupational therapist (even writing this it's just so crazy and ironic how this all happened). I often thought, *God, you already gave me so much empathy, I don't really need to go through more to know what others are dealing with. I kind of got this now.*

SETBACKS ALWAYS KEEP COMING

Did I think I could ever have a third stroke? Truth is, I never thought about it. I was too busy focusing on the life I was leading, the career I was building, and the dreams I was chasing. I was focused on invention, not discovery. I was inventing possibilities, inventing career moves, and inventing ideas around what perfect relationships looked like. I was traveling with the Phoenix Suns as their mental conditioning coach. The season had just ended, and I was thinking about what great things we could do and build on for next season. Again, I felt like I had hit my stride in life, and then I got knocked down *again*.

Stroke number three pretended to be a migraine at first. For a week, I muscled through a migraine that wouldn't go away. I had clients and meetings and people who were counting on me to show up. My activity calendar was full. By Thursday night, I couldn't sleep. I'd never experienced pain like that before in my entire life. I had one more meeting to get through on that Friday, so I focused on how I could make the meeting, despite the pain, and then crawl back into bed.

I made it through the meeting, barely. Stepping out of the office after the meeting, I was staggering. If you saw me, you'd think I'd had one too many drinks by the way I was weaving left to right down the hallway. Miraculously, I found my way to a clinic on the corner. They'd seen me before.

"Dar, we don't take your insurance," they told me. "But you're having a stroke. Let us call you an ambulance."

"Heck no," I said, knowing that would run me thousands of dollars.

Instead, I got myself an Uber. I think this is a good place to pause and say, I don't necessarily recommend this course of action if your brain is oxygen-starved, but it made perfect sense to me in the chaos of the moment. I was so focused on activity that even getting to an emergency room was about action only.

Don't worry, I told myself. The doctor at the clinic had handed me a note that read, *I'm having a stroke*, in case I became incapacitated before I reached the other hospital.

"Hey, I hope your friend's OK," the Uber driver said when he dropped me off. Even then I didn't want to worry anyone, so I didn't tell him that I thought I was having a stroke. I just walked into the emergency room.

I got into the emergency room and handed the receptionist my note. Fear washed across the girl's face. "Um, please have a seat," she said. I had no other options but to wait. My mother had just had her own stroke one month prior, so I didn't want to call my family in Connecticut and become another burden. I watched the doctors scurrying in and out of rooms, glancing back at me with varying degrees of panic. I thought, *No one I love is going to even know where I'm at if things go south.*

The nurses, their faces, and the thought I'd die alone are the last things I remember before waking up in a hospital bed . . . again.

My eyes immediately found the heart rate monitor. Up, down, up, down, up, down. All I could think was, *Please don't let me see that heartbeat go down.* I stared at that blue line moving in tandem with my pulse, as if my focus alone could be enough to keep it vacillating. *Do not flatline,* I told my body. *No flatlines.*

SETBACKS SUCK BUT PAVE NEW ROADS

In my career coaching professional athletes, I have come to know that injuries are a part of an athlete's life. Sometimes, an athlete suffers a career-threatening injury. Many players end their career with a major setback like an injury. To bounce back from a major injury when your physical body is your meal ticket requires a great deal of courage and determination. Some athletes, just like some humans, are born fighters and they etch their names into the history books with their spirits. It is the tremendous bounce backs from potentially career-ending injuries that push them into a higher status than the others.

You know Maria Sharapova as one of the top tennis players in the world. Back in 2008 she was in peak position, dominating every court, but luck wasn't on her side. Her setback showed up in the form of a shoulder injury so severe that it required surgery and took her off the courts for close to a year—a lifetime in a pro athlete's life.

But she recovered. She boldly stated that her career wasn't over and went on to complete her career at the Grand Slam in 2012 by winning the French Open.

The injury had some long-term effects on her playing style though. That's the thing about setbacks, not only do they suck, but they also rarely leave you the same as before. It was only due to her rigorous training and zeal to dominate that she was able to solidify such a great bounce back and move forward to regain and remain among the elite players in women's tennis.

And perhaps there is no more prominent story of bouncing back against the odds than Tiger Woods. One of the greatest players the sports world has ever seen with a massive list of achievements under his name but setbacks almost took it all away. In 2006, Tiger lost his father, who had been golfing with him since the age of two. In 2008, he suffered two stress fractures of the left tibia, which put him on six weeks' rest.

Next, TV screens mercilessly amplified his family issues and then in 2010, he and his then-wife Elin—who share two children together—divorced nearly six years after tying the knot. Soon, Tiger began to lose many of his big corporate sponsors. He opened the 2011 season with the Farmers Insurance Open and ended up in 44th place, marking his worst season opening of his career. In February 2011, Tiger's world ranking dropped to number 5. By November, his ranking had dropped to a career low of number 58. The legendary golfer had a winless streak that stretched out over 100 weeks, and it was clear his game and his psyche had been shaken by his public falling out over his personal scandals.

Tiger's entire life as a professional golfer has been a series of setbacks and bounce backs. Over the course of his career, Tiger underwent five back surgeries, five knee surgeries, an elbow injury, and numerous other physical issues. Most recently, he broke both of his legs after rolling his car in a serious single-vehicle accident in California in 2021. This setback occurred just a month after undergoing back surgery to correct a displaced disc.[1] Forced to undergo surgery to fix two fractures in his right leg and a shattered ankle after his accident, experts wondered if he would ever play pro golf again.

But he came roaring back, recapturing the world number 1 ranking. His numerous setbacks changed his path entirely and put him on a new path. As of this writing, Tiger has every big tournament title under his name with a chance to break Jack Niklaus's record of most majors won.

The point of both stories is that setbacks suck, but they can also help you come back stronger than ever and reset your life's path—help you reconnect to your purpose with a deeper commitment to greatness. And you don't have to be an elite athlete for this to happen. (See Figure 1.2.)

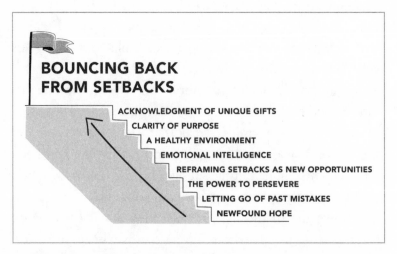

FIGURE 1.2. Bouncing back from setbacks helps you look toward higher ground with massive shifts in perspective. Success isn't defined by how many times you tumble down, but by how many times you take a step forward after getting back up.

Recognizing Setbacks That Challenge Your *Why Power*

Life is generous with setbacks. They can impact all areas of our life. For example:

Physically: You suffer an injury and you feel helpless.

Professionally: You experience job loss.

Personally: A hurricane levels your home and you lose everything.

Emotionally: Your mom dies.

Spiritually: Your church implodes with great division.

Relationally: You experience divorce.

Some of these are in your control, but most of them are not. All of them can challenge your commitment to your life's purpose.

OVERCOMING SETBACKS BY REFRAMING

What I can tell you from working through the setbacks I've shared in this chapter is that bouncing back is all about your ability to shift perspective and reframe the game as well as how quickly you can get back up. Whether a setback is because of a choice you made or the choices of someone else, the outcome depends on your ability to reframe it—and the speed in which you do so.

When we choose to dwell in the negative, it's a choice and will cause a reversal in our emotional/spiritual health journey. When someone else does something that interferes with our life, that's their choice. Yes, it's a setback for us, but we still hold the power of how we will respond and how fast the response will be. When you're slammed with a setback, remember: *success isn't defined by how many times you get knocked down, but by how many times you bounce back up and most important, how long it takes you to step forward.* We'll talk about this further in Principle 7.

THOUGHTS MATTER DURING A SETBACK

Remember, a setback is an interruption in progress, not an ending. See it as a comma, not a period. Our mindset will keep us moving forward in our purpose so we won't get stuck. What we pour into our minds and choose to rehearse in our thoughts makes a huge difference in being victorious despite setbacks.

12 Powerful Reframing Affirmations

With that in mind, here are 12 Powerful Reframing Affirmations you can use whenever you need them.

1. "Whatever is true, whatever is honorable, whatever is right, whatever is pure, whatever is lovely, whatever is of good repute, if there is any excellence and if anything worthy of praise, let your mind dwell on these things."—Philippians 4:8
2. To achieve massive success in my life and to achieve my most important goals, I must assume 100 percent responsibility for my life. Nothing less will do.
3. Even when you have doubts, take a step forward anyway. Take the chance because mistakes aren't failures, they are just new paths.
4. Failure is not fatal. I will survive this as I have survived all my past failures. I'm moving forward.

5. Giving up on the things that matter breeds weakness whereas trying again and again breeds strength.

6. What is meant to harm me will be turned to good. No attack spiritually, mentally, or emotionally will be successful in keeping me down.

7. I am committed to finding the lesson and something positive to focus on, no matter how negative the situation.

8. I am not lost in the mess of my setback. I see the big picture. This is temporary. The setback is setting me up for a comeback.

9. There is no failure only feedback.

10. A bad day does not mean a bad life.

11. It's OK to stop, to feel, to rest, to pause, to catch my breath, but then I must get up. I will not give up.

12. I am stronger than my current circumstances.

We are going to have months and even years that are setbacks, where we're working to regain traction in order to bounce back. And then we'll have months and years that are setups, where we've got momentum and forward motion. The seasons of descent and ascent go back-and-forth—that's just how life goes. The challenge for us is to learn how to surf the waves of life and move from setback to setup as quickly as possible, as often as possible.

To do this, you'll need to understand who you are. So let's get started.

PRINCIPLE 2

UNDERSTANDING WHO YOU ARE

The best moments in our lives are not the passive, receptive, relaxing times . . . The best moments usually occur if a person's body or mind is stretched to its limits in a voluntary effort to accomplish something difficult and worthwhile.
—Mihaly Csikszentmihalyi

No matter what the setback or who the person is, bouncing back from a bad situation and coming out stronger on the other side requires that we start with understanding who we are as individual humans. Adversity will never leave our lives entirely, which is what makes this principle so important. Over and over again, it works to recenter you around raising the bar and living a life in flow.

Understanding who you are is important when trying to achieve things you've never done before. It becomes the pathway for hitting your highest highs. In this chapter, I'll lay out why understanding your Fundamental Hardwiring and being *actively aware of your hardwiring* is the one-two punch you need to understand who you are and what drives you, holds you back, and keeps you focused on raising the bar in your life and others.

Discovering your Fundamental Hardwiring helps identify (maybe for the first time) the gifts, talents, and skill sets that help keep you in your personal best flow state. Having Active Awareness of your hardwiring helps you recognize when you are out of flow *and* identify the people, environments, and activities that support your best flow state.

FUNDAMENTAL HARDWIRING: UNDERSTANDING YOUR GIFTS AND HARNESSING THEM

Everybody is a genius. But if you judge a
fish by its ability to climb a tree, it will live
its whole life believing that it is stupid.
–Albert Einstein

I woke up one day and realized I was the fish from that Albert Einstein quote and running multiple companies felt like that tree. It's not that I'm stupid. It's the fact that I was going against my nature. At the time, I wasn't allowed to run the companies in the way I knew how. I was micromanaged and forced to do things that were not in line with my gifts. My genius was not being tapped into. Sure, I was making great money, but I could feel how out of alignment

I was, which led to me feeling like I was going through the motions instead of making a real impact. You can have all the accolades and money in the world, but if your work is not aligned to who you are and how you work best, it's going to feel like *work*. You will be left unhappy and just existing.

It wasn't until I met my mentor, Laurie Beth Jones, and took her assessment, the Path Elements Profile[1] (PEP), that the light bulb finally lit up. You've probably taken a similar assessment test like Myers Briggs, Enneagram, Culture Index, Predictive Index, Mercer Mettl, Chally, or another. All of them collect Fundamental Hardwiring data, which can then be used to measure and optimize your work, your life, and your performance—at work and at home.

The survey I took outlined that my personality was very specific, a "double wind archetype." It explained that I'm a creative force that while powerful and all-encompassing can be a little hard to ground. People like me are all about big ideas and propelling others forward in collaboration. We are big-picture and fast-moving thinkers with a relationship-oriented mindset, always striving to enhance opportunities and flow.

Wind types cannot be successful or happy if they are contained. They are vision setters and help people move toward the vision, so they reject being constrained. Laurie pointed out that the common denominator in all of my ventures was my passion for helping others. But as a wind type, I require a free spirit to propel big ideas forward. To teach, speak, coach, advise, lead others to a better way. With constraints I felt tense, disconnected, and anxious.

Once I understood these results, it was clear to me why my work wasn't working. Having the freedom to paint the big picture of the company fits my elemental flow but being micromanaged or handling the details and timeline constraints drains me. I finally understood my Fundamental Hardwiring, and that information would change my life and the lives of everyone I coached going forward.

Exercise: Personality Test

Go ahead and take whichever personality test you'd like from the options I shared earlier in this chapter. Take the time to review and understand your results. Doing so will allow you to understand yourself, how you can produce your best work, and how you work with others best. While each has differences, the main results are pretty similar and give you a great understanding of who you are.

IDENTIFYING YOUR FUNDAMENTAL HARDWIRING

If someone isn't wired to network and hates talking to people, putting them in sales will lead to missed sales quotas, smaller contracts, and stunted growth. You would never put a pro baseball player who loves driving results in the field at a desk job doing Excel spreadsheets. It's impossible to hit it out of the park when our gifts, talents, and skills are not properly used.

Many times in business, people are judged and labeled based on their performance in a particular role. But if their job was not set up with their ideal workflow state in mind, everyone's time and money will be wasted. Leaders who don't understand the power of knowing their team's Fundamental Hardwiring will put just anyone in charge and say, "I want you to run this department," or "I want to give you an aggressive bonus plan"—and then wonder why those people hate their jobs and experience failure. Now that you understand the key role Fundamental Hardwiring plays in happiness and success, it's easy for you to see why they would get rattled and lose their confidence. The job was never actually cut out for them. They were set up for everything but success.

The most successful companies in the world understand the performance advantage that personality assessments provide. In fact, according to *Psychology Today*, approximately 80 percent of Fortune 500 companies use these tests to assess, hire, and incentivize employees.[2] With a statistic like that, it is likely you've actually taken one of these personality assessments in your career. And if you lead an organization, it would not be surprising if you used one currently to guide employee acquisition and performance evaluations. While there is much debate as to which of the personality assessments is the most accurate as a diagnostic tool, the point is that the results that allow you to understand your own or an employee's Fundamental Hardwiring are valid and useful, especially when trying to achieve optimal performance.

Why are they so beneficial? Because the information from the assessment can be used to increase individual self-awareness and professional development. It also improves the strategic development of the organization.

And I can speak from my own experience and those of my clients, understanding your hardwiring helps you see what wasn't working in past and current ventures. It helps you frame the kind of people you should surround yourself with to create your best performance and team dynamic. It also highlights blind spots. And this was the most important for me: it gives you the vocabulary you need to communicate to others what you need to produce your best.

Once I understood my Fundamental Hardwiring, instead of finding myself running a set of companies in a role bogged down by restraints on my creativity and communication skills, I was free to pursue a life that inspired me and led to my best work. (See Figure 2.1.)

FIGURE 2.1. Your Fundamental Hardwiring is the core of who you are. From that center, your gifts, skills, and talents are formed. By having an Active Awareness of your Fundamental Hardwiring as well as your gifts, skills, and talents, you can effectively understand who you are and communicate to others the best way to activate your flow state.

Now it's time to understand how to put this knowledge into practice and make all of that your new reality.

How Do You Use Fundamental Hardwiring?

Once you understand your *Fundamental Hardwiring,* this information can and should be used to inform every aspect of your daily choices—where you work, who you surround yourself with, what goals you set, what you agree to, and how you structure your day. And most important, how you find your favorite lane and stay in it.

So how do you start using this information every day? One tool I like to share about with my clients is Active Awareness. Active Awareness is the awareness of your surroundings, circumstances, and thoughts in a way that allows you to be in control of your reactions, no matter the situation. Examples include noticing how you respond to sudden situations (calm or anxious), being conscious of your mindset throughout the day (positive self-talk or negative), and how you listen to other people when they are speaking (open-minded or confrontational). Not surprisingly, Active Awareness is related to improved athletic performance and the propensity to achieve flow states. While the research here is more recent, the relationship between Active Awareness and flow is very strong; both are beneficial states of mind. Flow involves losing self-awareness within an activity. Active Awareness involves maintaining self-awareness throughout or despite an activity. The relationship is well studied.[3]

But what does Active Awareness mean to you and your hardwiring?

If the ultimate goal of this book is to help you achieve greatness in every area of your life, then Active Awareness is what allows you to tap into your hardwiring so you can reach greatness. It's what helps you get centered during adversity, trauma, setbacks, or plateaus.

If you're operating in a capacity that's outside of your natural hardwiring and skill sets, you're probably miserable. You're probably stagnant. Active Awareness of your Fundamental Hardwiring will allow you to recognize this; see that you aren't utilizing your specific gifts, talents, and drivers; and set you up to figure out what you need to achieve greatness in your role—or find one that does that for you.

When I got my assessment results back and I began to understand my Fundamental Hardwiring, everything clicked into place for me. I was now actively aware of my Fundamental Hardwiring. I understood my source of greatness, my capacity to use my gifts to help others, and my ability to bounce back. I started to surround myself with people who supported my archetype. And I finally found myself being able to accept my wiring instead of wishing I were different, like I had been doing my whole life.

And that brings up an important point. When you are feeling like you've hit a wall or plateau or like you aren't aligned with your Fundamental Hardwiring, do a gut check and ask yourself these prompting questions:

- Do I have a clear understanding of the task at hand and clear goals for completion?
- Are my skills and strengths a match for the task at hand?
- Do my activities align with my hardwiring?

- Am I in a situation that I should have said "no" to?
- Is there a communication barrier as a result of different personality types that is disrupting the flow of everyone involved?
  - How can that be rectified?
  - Have I clearly communicated with my team how I operate?

When you answer these questions using Active Awareness, it forces you to connect your Fundamental Hardwiring to the activities or the situations you're in. When you go against your Fundamental Hardwiring, succeeding at tasks, goals, conversations, problem solving, and even keeping a positive mindset becomes difficult and taxing. Looking through the lens of these questions you can pinpoint where the disconnect is, fix it, and move forward with more clarity.

PUTTING IT ALL TOGETHER

Here's where you might be thinking, "This is all great and well, Dar, but what does being actively aware of your hardwiring have to do with bouncing back?"

No matter what setback you've faced, you cannot bounce back from it and move forward unless you:

- Understand your Fundamental Hardwiring, which acknowledges your gifts, talents, and skills (the very things you'll use to move forward)—this is where the assessments come in.

- Apply your Fundamental Hardwiring from the assessment to the activities in your life (work, family, personal) so that you are engaged and excited about them—this is where Active Awareness comes in.
- Take action after a setback to move forward (easier when you are not working against your hardwiring) by making meaningful decisions—this is where flow comes in.

Outside of growing in self-awareness, understanding your Fundamental Hardwiring allows you to become mindful of what works for you and what doesn't. What activities and people inspire you and which ones drain you. What kind of situations allow you to shine, and which turn you into a nervous wreck. Becoming more aware of your gifts, talents, and skill sets helps you make key choices in how you live each day and where and who you invest your energy in. Becoming aware helps guide your conversations and decisions in a way that supports your ability to get into flow and stay in flow because you safeguard against things that move you away from your best performance.

But how do you access your Fundamental Hardwiring if you are in pain, mentally drained, feeling hopeless, or any combination of negative emotions? How do you see the forest through the trees when you feel paralyzed by your setback—even with this knowledge? The answer is simple although hard for many: Seek Feedback, and this is the next principle we'll dive into together now.

SEEKING AND APPLYING FEEDBACK

Feedback is the breakfast of champions.
–Ken Blanchard

There you are, living your best life and being in flow when *bam*—suddenly you lose that flow along with your confidence and resilience.

A setback can happen in a moment and last a long time. From the perspective of pro athletes, losing your flow is an easy thing to do. One day you're making the shot from the 3-point line, and the next day you can't hit the rim anywhere on the court. I coach a professional basketball player, we'll call Sam for privacy reasons. Our conversation during a coaching session went something like this:

Sam: I think I've lost my edge. I don't think I'm good enough to be on the team with the other players in the league anymore.

Dar: What has changed?

Sam: I don't know. I just don't have it anymore. All the papers, the TV, the networks . . . they are all seeing it. It's gone. My confidence . . .

Dar: OK. Let's get centered. You have to refocus your energy on a different narrative. You know what you are good at—what makes you great in this game. If I'm a scout, what would I write on your scorecard? What makes you great at this sport and got you where you are today?

Sam: What got me here? That's easy . . .

Of course, he immediately had the answer! He knew his skills on the court better than the back of his own hand. I made Sam write those skills down and rank them the way a talent scout might. When he showed me his skill set list, I said, "Perfect. Now, what I want you to do is watch a video of yourself doing those things. I want you to see yourself in this flow state so, when you get back on the court for a big game, you can reproduce this and tune out all of your self-doubt. Once you get momentum going and take your power back from the naysayers, you will be able to access your flow again."

This technique of writing down your skills is so vital to finding your flow once you've lost it. It is a refocusing tool that forces you to remember both your people data and how your gifts, talents, and skills show up in the world when you are doing what you love. And it's one I would highly recommend you do right now.

Once you do this, you'll be set up to tune back into who you are and the skills that you do have—versus focusing on your weaknesses when you're not in your flow. Think about it! If you're in a space where your skills aren't being utilized to their full potential or you're working in a way that goes against your flow, of course you're going to be convinced that you're bad at something! By having this player get reconnected with his skills and watch video of himself performing in that flow state over and over so he can perfectly practice those skills when crunch time came, he was able to shake his doubts, tune out the noise, and perform at his peak!

In the work environment, this technique can also be very useful when coaching an employee through a setback, like missing a sales goal, not closing the big client, or falling short in leading their team. The conversation can go something like this:

Employee: I'm not sure what's happening. I'm not sure why I can't drive the results I used to. Nothing is working anymore.

You: What has changed?

Employee: I don't know. But everything seems harder. The deck is stacked against me . . .

You: OK. Let's get centered. You have to refocus your energy on a different narrative. You know what you are good at—what made us hire and promote you? If I'm a recruiter, what would I tell other employers about why you're such a great hire? What can you bring to our organization that others cannot? What got you into this position in the first place?

Employee: What got me here? Well, I know that . . .

Exercise: Confidence Card

When I coach people one-to-one to help them push through mental roadblocks after a setback, I do an exercise with them that is incredibly effective because it acts like a mirror. Since you've already identified your Fundamental Hardwiring, you have everything you need to do this exercise yourself.

Send an email to three to five people in your world asking for their feedback around your gifts and talents. Make it fair by asking people from every environment of your life. Ask people who see you every day at work, at home, friends, family, people who work above you, and people who work below you. People in your life notice your patterns of behavior and the places that you shine. Synthesize their responses by paying attention to what's repeated.

The email can be very simple.

Hello _____ ,

I'm doing leadership development work and would appreciate your candid response to these questions.

If you were to write a paragraph or two describing me, what would you say?

Who would you say I am?

What would you say I am really good at?

Can you list my two to three most prominent skills?

I'm grateful for you in my life.

Best,

Your name

> Once you get the responses back, sit down and circle the common themes from the responses. Did everybody say you're a good listener? Did everybody say you're innovative? Did everybody say you're a hard worker?

The goal of this exercise is to find the common denominators and use them to hone in on the DNA of what puts you into flow. Those are your gifts. Once you know your wiring and gifts, you can start aligning your life with them by what you agree to and what you don't agree to.

Finally, write down the most common words on an index card. This is now your Confidence Card. This simple card has helped my clients remember what makes them great in all kinds of circumstances. It becomes a source of power whenever you need it.

I once did a live version of this practice with an audience member during a speech. I called up a woman on stage and asked her simply, "Do you ever doubt yourself?" Her answer? "All the time." I then asked her, "What are the things you doubt yourself in?" She explained all the things and then I asked her what she does. She shared that she was a singer.

Knowing all of that, I then turned to get the audience involved. I asked them if anyone knew her, and almost everyone in the room raised their hand. I then asked the crowd, "Would you ever think she thought these things about herself?" In unison, the room said, "No!" I then asked people in the audience to just start yelling out what makes the woman standing next to me so great, and I started to write down their answers. After just a few minutes, we had a page filled with all the things that made her amazing. I then gave her that paper and asked her to read it with "I am . . ." before each word or phrase. With each word, the smile on her face grew bigger and bigger. At the end, she gave me the biggest hug and cried. I looked at her in front of an audience full of people supporting her and said, "This is you. This is who you are and don't ever forget that. But, if you do, look back at this."

That is the power of the Confidence Card. This exercise is also a form of feedback, which is crucial to excelling.

WATCHING FILM: IDENTIFYING WHAT FLOW LOOKS LIKE FOR YOU

Perhaps one of the best examples of seeking feedback to become a champion is one of the most loved, gifted, and arguably the best basketball players of all time, Kobe Bryant.

Bryant was a self-professed game film "nerd." He started watching film when he was a kid—studying the greats and the game in tandem. "Film study is all about detail," said Bryant. "From a young age—a very young age—I devoured film and watched everything I could get my hands on. It was always fun to me. Some people, after all, enjoy looking at a watch; others are happier figuring out how the watch works. It was always fun to watch, study, and ask myself the most important question: 'Why?'"[1]

As Bryant grew as a player, his skills as a student of game film grew as well. ". . . I went from watching what was there to watching for what was missing and should have been there. I went from watching what happened to what could have and should have happened. Film study eventually became imagining alternatives, counters, options, in addition to the finite details of why some actions work and others don't work."[2]

Bryant said that by studying game film, he trained his mind to stay in a state of flow on and off the court by focusing on and studying every detail of his life. Watching our own "game" film helps us stay in flow in business and in life.

● ● ●

I grew up in Connecticut in a very Italian, East Coast family. Every single Sunday during football season we'd go to church, all my aunts and uncles would come over, we'd eat a huge Italian meal, and we'd watch the New York Giants. Then on Wednesdays, my uncles would come back over, we'd pop in a VHS that my dad had taped of the game, and we'd literally rewatch film, breaking down the plays and body language of the guys. We'd do this for UConn games and the Yankees, too. We would analyze the film and talk through the different strategies we saw teams implementing and how their approach was either spot-on or how they could have managed the game better. We were some ruthless couch coaches.

I've been *watching film* for almost 40 years.

When it came time for me to play field hockey in school, my dad knew nothing about the game, so he went out and got tapes to learn how it's played. Yes, this is the kind of dad I had, and he said, "the more we know, the more we improve at our craft," which made such a difference. We'd watch instructional videos together and even films of other games and players, further instilling in me this idea that there's wisdom *and* knowledge to be gained from watching film.

Here's the thing about watching films. Watching films requires emotional intelligence. When watching film for any sport, you need to have the knowledge to actually see what worked and what didn't right away in order to adjust and innovate for the next game. Watching films is a way to seek feedback on your own life—feedback from others and from yourself. There's no space for defensiveness in this practice. We can apply a filter to feedback as part of our game film process.

I've been using many sports examples up until now because they are easy to grasp, but you can watch film in any situation. What does it look like when you are leading a company meeting? What does flow look like when you are hitting your goals? What patterns begin to pop up when you lose your confidence and start to fall out of flow?

Do you record your company meetings? Do you record yourself giving live talks? Do you record your creative process? Not everything has to be captured in video; in fact, here's an exercise that will give you the same feedback you'd get if you were watching film—but no video of your life is required.

Exercise: Seeking Feedback to Comeback

Here are a few suggestions to make soliciting feedback part of your regular routine:

- Once a month, send a text to three to five people you interact with socially. Ask the following questions:
  - What's it like to be on the other side of me?
  - What's something I'm saying a lot lately?
  - What's one way I could improve my work or personal life?

- Once a quarter, send out a Google form or any anonymous inquiry form to these same people *and* two to three people you work with and ask the following:
  - How do people describe me when I'm not in the room?
  - How do you feel when the phone rings or dings and my name is on the screen?
  - What do you understand to be my current goals?
  - What advice would you give me right now?

- If you run a business or organization, twice a year, send out an in-depth feedback analysis to at least 10 people from every environment of your life (work, home, clubs, teams, etc.). Examples can include:
  - 360-degree feedback
  - Workhuman Conversations
  - Lattice

> - At the end of each day, do a self-reflection exercise. The following questions will help you mentally watch film from your day so you can note in real time what you want to change; that way, you don't let too much time go by before you adjust. Doing this sets you up for operating like a pro. Remember you are the pro of your life, so start creating daily habits like this one. And answer these questions before bed each day:
>   ◦ What were my wins today?
>   ◦ What were my challenges today?
>   ◦ What are my areas of improvement based on the day?

Feedback is incredibly valuable, but for it to be useful, you have to deeply understand it. For any feedback you receive, ask the following filtering questions:

- Do I fully understand this feedback, or do I need more details before processing it?
- What happens if I do nothing in reaction to this feedback?
- What happens if I take action in reaction to this feedback?
- Is this feedback something I've heard before?
- How could this feedback help me level up?

We've got to mentally train ourselves to not just withstand scrutiny, but to seek it out. To look for it. Too long for it. Because it sharpens and refines us in ways that no other practice will. Why? Someone else's experience of you is different from your perspective of that experience. Another way to explain this dynamic is by thinking about angles. In sports, there are cameras strategically set up all over stadiums and coliseums, not to film the game for entertainment, but to catch certain angles of play.

What looks to be a clean defensive play from one angle can be shown as a blatant foul from another. If you're not getting a 360-degree evaluation of yourself, you're not operating with all the information. You're operating on a partial perspective. We've all got blind spots. This is why learning to watch film is critical to identifying what you look and act like when you are in flow and what patterns you exhibit when you fall out of flow.

One of the biggest reasons people get stuck after a setback is because they are defensive about the changes that need to occur in order for them to bounce back and move forward. One of the purposes of watching films is so you and others can recognize patterns of behavior—positive and negative—and then move forward repeating only the moments of greatness. A key component to finding your flow is to eliminate defensive behaviors that hold you in place after a setback.

ELIMINATING DEFENSES
TO BOUNCE BACK

Companies bring me in to coach their employees on mindset, mind power, and mental agility because they recognize feedback and training is missing from their internal HR practices. Think about it: most people wait for a performance review once a year. Just *one* time a year, employees receive feedback. And many clients I've coached have walked away from a performance review ready to quit. They have a complete breakdown or get defensive and pissed off. The reaction comes from three places.

First, the person conducting the performance review is not trained on how to communicate to people's individual archetypes. Second, the employee has no training on how to receive feedback and coaching. Three is the realization that you should be getting feedback more than once a year.

If you were a professional athlete, you'd get every swing, every throw, every pass, every shot, every move you make reviewed by your coaches, teammates, the media, other players, the fans, and critics. Athletes need to be able to receive the scrutiny and process that in a way that is productive, not destructive. Imagine if you walked out of a meeting and opened your phone to find thousands of tweets about how well or how poorly you managed your team that day.

Now you might say, "Dar, I'm not a professional athlete. They get paid to take that kind of heat—I don't." I'm not talking about money. I'm talking about greatness. And if you don't want to be great, respectfully, why are you reading this book? Feedback is fundamental to growth and in turn, greatness. Flinders University published a study in 2020 on the science of defensiveness and the effects defensiveness has on our problem solving. "Defensive responses to transgressions undermine our ability to identify a problem correctly and act to solve it, negatively impacting decision-making within government and organizations, in relationships, and even in relation to our own individual well-being." Ultimately, the study concluded that "defensiveness creates blind spots in decision-making." When a person or group reacts to feedback defensively, "problems go unrecognized, victims go unacknowledged, and relationships deteriorate."[3]

It's OK to acknowledge that hearing difficult things about yourself is not what any of us would call a good time. But as Robert Allen would say, "There is no failure. Only feedback."

DISCOVERING YOUR WHY POWER

Finding why *is a process of discovery,*
not invention.
—Simon Sinek

I opened the first chapter of this book by sharing that my second thought every morning is the possibility that a fourth stroke could render me without the ability to speak ever again—or worse. Will I have a fourth stroke? I hate to admit it, but the odds are not in my favor. This single fact is why I am so committed to my Why Power on a daily basis. I have to help people today because my tomorrow is not promised.

Your Why Power is made up of two things: your Mission Statement and your Power Word. Together, these tools will sustain you far longer than willpower ever could. You see, so often people want to will themselves through situations, but that's not sustainable, especially in tough times. But having a mission to follow and align with is sustainable and will keep you motivated far beyond any adversity you hit. Willpower doesn't get you through hard times. Why Power does.

Why Power summaries *why* you are driven to do what you do and elevates your performance by helping you show-case your gifts, talents, and skills. Once you do this work to discover your Why Power (and we will in this chapter), you can create powerful changes and impact in every area of your life. On a personal level, this helps you create a life that is not only rewarding but fulfilling. On a professional level, this helps you spend your time on the tasks that really make you thrive and find your flow. On a team level, fueling other people's Why Power creates stronger teams, bigger results, and the ability to scale success faster.

DISCOVERING YOUR WHY POWER

In order to really use your Why Power in any situation, whether it's a setback, challenge, or exciting moment in your life, you first need to have a clear Mission Statement and Power Word. Together, these two tools will help you get through any setback, big or small.

The goal of your Mission Statement is to guide you, help you align with the things that matter to you, and give you clarity on the things that don't. Much like a business makes all decisions around their mission, so should you. One thing to call out now is that many people use different terms for "mission." Whether you use the word or phrase "purpose," "life's intention," or "life's work" does not matter. All that matters is that your statement captures why you do what you do.

The goal of your Power Word (which, as the name suggests, is just one word) is to inspire you and be a quick jolt whenever you need a reminder of why you're doing what you're doing. This word will basically act as your own personal bumper sticker that clearly says to anyone who sees it, "This why I do what I do." That being said, it's also important to remember that your Mission Statement and Power Word should never be based on a role or currently held title. Your Why Power is much deeper than any one role.

To give you an example, my Mission Statement is *My why is to inspire, empower, and awaken greatness in myself and others globally.*

My Power Word is *Greatness.*

To give you an example of just how powerful your Mission Statement can be, I'd like to share a story from one of my clients.

Power of a Mission Statement

Several years ago I found myself at a crossroads. My husband and I were about to make a major transition away from a startup we helped to grow. We'd put our heart and soul into building it, and while we loved the work we were doing, it didn't come without sacrifice.

53

The day we knew we had to make a change started like any other. We woke up, got ready, shuffled our kids off to school, and worked a long day at the office. Later that evening, as we got ready for bed, my husband looked me in the eyes and asked me if I knew what the day before was.

"The day before?" *Hmmm* . . . I thought for a moment but came up short.

"What was yesterday's date?" I asked.

"July 15th."

My jaw dropped in disbelief. It was our anniversary—a fact that didn't register with either one of us until a full day later.

Now while I've heard of one spouse accidentally forgetting an anniversary, I've never heard of it happening to both before. And the truth of the matter is that it wasn't because we didn't care—we had just become too overloaded and laser-focused on growing our company that most other things had taken a back seat out of necessity. This, however, was a major wake-up call.

This was the moment we knew we had to make a change. While we knew in our hearts that it was the right move, what would come next was a big unknown. I'll never forget the day things started to come into focus.

Dar and I sat across from one another in a crowded restaurant, and she asked what the future held. I shared my heart with her and talked about the things I'm most passionate about. I can't recall exactly what I said, but I remember feeling a mix of both optimism and uncertainty.

Right then and there, in the middle of the busy restaurant, Dar encouraged me to craft my Mission Statement. So we grabbed a cocktail napkin, borrowed a pen from the server, and got started. What came out next has been one of the greatest blessings and something that has helped guide countless decisions since. My Mission Statement is now the measure by which I choose to take something on or to let it fall by the wayside. It's helped me say both yes and no with clarity and conviction.

It's hard to believe that something so simple could be so significant, but what I've come to realize is that there is immeasurable power in understanding our purpose here on Earth. Life doesn't come with a road map, but once we tap into what we're here to do, the path ahead becomes much clearer, and decisions can be made with certainty.

Your Mission Statement and Power Word have the power to change your life. And that may sound like a big promise, but as you can see from that story, it's the truth. So let's get to work on crafting your personal Mission Statement and Power Word in just three steps. (See Figure 4.1.)

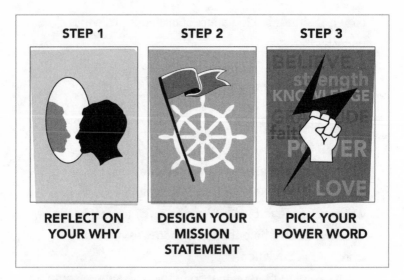

FIGURE 4.1. To discover your Why Power, you have to follow these three steps. Reflecting on what your Why encompasses lays the foundation for your Mission Statement, which you then compress into your one Power Word.

Step 1: Reflect on Your Why

Understanding your Why is a big task, so let's work through a few different exercises and related questions to do this together:

- Imagine your own *30 for 30* or the toast that people will give at your 100th birthday:
  - What do you want people to say about you?
  - What do you want to have accomplished by the time you're 100?
  - What do you want to be remembered for?

- Think on how your life experiences have informed your passion:
  - What are you most passionate about?
  - What five specific experiences in your life have made you feel the most proud and felt the most meaningful?
  - How have these life experiences fueled you to get you to where you are today?

- Research core values: Core values are your anchors, they represent your highest priorities, deeply held beliefs, and core, fundamental driving forces. Examples of core values include integrity, respect, responsibility, sportsmanship, and servant leadership. Go ahead and look up a list of additional core values and then ask yourself:
  - What five core values stick out to you the most?
  - Why do these five feel so meaningful to you?
  - If your life was to operate on these five guiding core values, would you be proud of them?

The answers to these sets of questions should help you understand more about what motivates you and who you want to be.

Step 2: Design Your Mission Statement

Now that you're a little clearer on what motivates you, it's time to actually create your Mission Statement.

To get started, fill in the following sentence:

My Why is to _____

_____.

Take your time with this. Have your mission fit into one sentence. The simpler it is, the easier it is to recall and live by.

Go ahead and rewrite and fill this in as many times as you need. This statement should be one that truly reflects why you get up every morning and what gives your life meaning—so do the work to give it the time and attention it deserves.

As a reminder, my Mission Statement is

> *My Why is to inspire, empower, and awaken greatness in myself and others globally.*

Some other examples include:

> *My Why is to add value in the lives of others.*

> *My mission is to leave people better than I found them.*

> *My purpose is to create better leaders.*

> *My life's intention is to leave a legacy of impact.*

> *My life's work is to help others tell their story.*

When I coach pro athletes and high-powered CEOs, I always ask them to do this work and create their own Mission Statement because it's directly tied to maintaining your state of flow. You cannot get back into flow if you are not clear on the why behind your actions and the work you are doing to raise the bar in your own life and the lives of others!

Step 3: Pick Your Power Word

Now it's time to get your Mission Statement down to just one word to uncover your Power Word.

What one word in your Mission Statement really reflects who you are and who you want to be? That word will be your Power Word.

Using the Why Power statements we just looked at earlier, let's look at the Why Power Word that could be used for each sentence:

> **Mission Statement:** *My Why is to add value in the lives of others.*
> **Power Word:** *Value*

> **Mission Statement:** *My mission is to leave people better than I found them.*
> **Power Word:** *Improvement*

> **Mission Statement:** *My purpose is to create better leaders.*
> **Power Word:** *Lead*

Mission Statement: *My life's intention is to leave a legacy of impact.*
Power Word: *Impact*

Mission Statement: *My life's work is to help others tell their story.*
Power Word: *Storytelling*

Once you've chosen your word, write it down on a notecard, make it the background of your phone, or put it on a sticky note that you leave on your bathroom mirror. Whatever you do, make sure that word is also visible to you, so when life (or someone) knocks you off your game and out of your state of flow, you can rely on your Why to bounce back even better. Your Power Word is like your life's anthem song. When it comes on, you get excited.

Now celebrate yourself for all of the hard work you just did to set yourself up for success going forward! Great work!

WHY POWER AND SETBACKS

Once you have a clear Mission Statement and Power Word, you will have your Why Power. With your Why Power defined, setbacks will feel more like a bump in the road rather than a dead end because we have the fuel to put action into motion. When we know our Why, we are able to overcome any setback that comes our way—whether that's a bad game or season for an athlete, a missed promotion that would propel a career professional forward, a major hit to the success of a business in the wake of a worldwide pandemic, or a health emergency that leaves your sense of self rattled. Because of the work you've done, you will be able to bounce back and level up better than ever because you know there is something bigger than your ego driving you.

In fact, with your Why Power, setbacks provide the opportunity for rediscovering your positive mindset, clarity, joy, and resilience. And you can power through those setbacks because you can recognize the obstacle for what it is: *an opportunity*.

Recently, one of my clients went through a situation where he experienced a major setback, but instead of that dragging him down, he used his Why Power to see the situation as an opportunity.

This client once played for the New York Yankees, and after his professional baseball career, he worked in the front office as a scout for a major league sports team. At the time, he was also entertaining aspirations of becoming a general manager (GM).

As part of our work together, he created a Mission Statement and Power Word to get super clear on his Why Power. After all of the great work he did, he shared his goal to become a GM with his boss.

The reaction he got shocked him—and me. My client's boss took offense at his aspirations and lashed out at him in a totally inappropriate way.

After the conversation, my client called me and shared what happened.

"I'm so sorry," I said. "That wasn't right. Are you OK?"

"I am," he replied. "It's surprising, because normally, a reaction like his would have crushed me. But because I know my gifts, I know my talents, I know my Why, it didn't rattle me like it normally would have." He added, "Honestly, Dar, this is a wake-up call. If this is how this organization is going to treat me, I don't want to work for them."

His ability to bounce back from that attack spoke volumes. Because he knew his Why Power so firmly, what someone else said about him didn't automatically become "true." He may have heard his boss's words and they may have hurt, but they didn't stick to him and he was able to use this setback as an opportunity.

Not long after this conversation, my client got a call from a prominent MLB team to work in their front office. I wasn't sure what he was going to do—and he wasn't either. But after thinking it through for a bit, he shared this with me: "I thought I wanted to be a GM. But I think I'm going to go and become a financial advisor and work for my father's financial advisement firm."

"Wow," I said. "Tell me about that decision."

"Through figuring out my Mission Statement and Power Word, I learned so much about how important work life-harmony is to me and I'm crystal clear on my Why Power. Neither this new opportunity nor my current job align with that or where I thought I was going. So instead I'm going to completely change my career."

And he did. My client is so much happier now as a financial advisor. He's no longer on the road chasing talent or wins; instead he gets to see his kids every morning and night. If he didn't have the mental foundation, the confidence to go after what was truly important to him, and the deep understanding of who he truly was that comes from your Why Power, he wouldn't be where he is today.

• • •

Knowing your Why Power allows you to see each decision you make through a microscope. It gives you this clarity so that lows are not low lows. And what's normally scary is not anymore because your foundation is solid. The storms in life will come. You'll get rained on. The winds will blow. But you won't be moved or crippled or knocked down because what you're standing on is the sturdy knowledge of what makes you *you*, which makes you unshakable.

Think of all that you've been through up until this moment. You've conquered incredible feats and slayed countless dragons in your way. This alone should prove to you that you can accomplish anything. When we give up on our dreams and goals, it's not because we don't have the time. It's because our Why isn't big enough. Now that will never be the case because you're set up to live your life with intentional and purposeful actions.

CREATING YOUR BOUNCE BACK ENVIRONMENT

At first, you might find that nothing happens there.
But if you have a sacred space and use it, eventually,
something will happen. Your sacred space is
where you find yourself again and again.
—Joseph Campbell

Have you ever tried to get into a great mood amid the chaos? Mental chaos shows up differently in everyone's life. For some, having a dirty or disorganized home creates mental chaos. For others, loud noises and crowds create mental chaos. And then there are those people who find mental chaos in unfamiliar places. Whatever causes it for you, the fact is that mental chaos keeps us in setback mode. The environments you surround yourself with (including people) determine Mental Chaos. This may sound overly simple, but it is powerful.

You're now familiar with the importance of your Fundamental Hardwiring, and believe it or not, this plays a critical role in what environment you work best in, too. Think about it this way. If you're someone who seeks out details, facts, and structure, a cluttered office or home environment will not be a space that helps you do your best work and find your flow.

Or perhaps you find your flow when things are not rushed and when you have time to reflect. You likely prefer quiet places and to be around people that respect your soft nature. Can you imagine getting into your flow and achieving your best results in an office environment that is loud and filled with toxic people?

With these examples in mind, it's easy to see why understanding your Fundamental Hardwiring is crucial to keeping yourself in flow and focused on your Why Power—both of which are keys to bouncing back from setbacks. So being more intentional about the environments you surround yourself with is a must. This chapter will help you do exactly that by understanding the importance of your Bounce Back Environments.

DEFINING BOUNCE BACK ENVIRONMENTS

What we see and experience in our environments is deeply connected to how we feel, think, and perform. Take a look around you now. Where are you? What does your space look like? What do you see, feel, hear, taste, and smell? All of this can positively or negatively affect your flow and ability to reach your greatness.

Another important question to ask yourself is "*Who* is around you?" The people in your life are part of your environment, too. We rise or fall to the level of the people around us. I'm always around people who are optimizers in all areas of their life because I always want to level up myself. I challenge myself to be around those who do great things because I want to continue to do great things.

If you're not surrounding yourself with high-caliber people, how do you ever expect to become a quality, high-caliber person? If you want a better life, spend time with people who fit your future version and bring out the best in you.

Think about your environment this way. Imagine that you are a big receptacle. You receive information all day through your different environments (and your senses, which we'll get to later). Over time, the combined effects of that input make that receptacle either heavier or lighter. Think about the relationship factors alone that can impact how heavy or light you feel:

- What's the quality of people you spend time with?
  - Toxic or narcissistic?
  - Unmotivated or victim card players?
  - Self-pitying or complaint driven?
  - Pessimistic or negative?
  - Happy and full of ideas?
  - Inspiring and motivating?
  - Supportive and solution driven?
  - Optimistic and positive?

- Who do you take advice from?
  - People who have achieved the level of success you are seeking?
  - People who have negative or cynical mindsets?
  - People with an agenda?
  - People with formal training in the subject matters?

- How much time do you spend watching or reading the news every day?
  - Are you adding to your knowledge base with great books and inspired content?
  - Are you reading negative news with an agenda?

An environment is any place we are and any conditions in which we exist, especially the people, places, and things we encounter regularly and intentionally. When I coach people, they often relapse by getting disconnected from their Why Power and losing their flow because they are in an environment that doesn't support their greatness.

Meet "Cathy"

One of my CEO clients, we'll call her Cathy, brought me in for mental edge coaching because she was having a ton of trouble getting into her flow. She struggled with reactiveness and found herself involved in a lot of personal and professional drama, disrupting her mental state and, as a result, her team's productivity.

As we went through my coaching system, Principles 1 to 4 were easy for Cathy to identify. During Principle 6,

Emotional Intelligence, which we will cover in the next chapter, we got stuck, and then Cathy started going backward in the coaching. It hit me like a slap upside the head. I realized that I hadn't yet taken the time to assess her environment thoroughly. Not just her desk but her home and car as well. We were hitting roadblocks in her progress because things in her life were chaotic.

This brilliant leader was experiencing so much mental chaos because she wasn't prioritizing the tidiness of her spaces or the people around her. We've all had points where clutter starts to take over, but how long we stay in those cluttered spaces impacts us in many ways. The places where she went for relaxation and solace—the sacred spaces Joseph Campbell speaks of—were overflowing with disorganization. She never allowed herself to fully step away from the stressors that kept her *reactive* instead of *reflective*.

I told her, "We can work on your emotional intelligence all day, but we *have* to get you into a truly supportive environment. This includes creating a routine of organization and tidiness *and* cutting out some of the unhealthy people around you who are adding to the chaos and drama in your life. If you want to take a breath, you need to do everything you can to stop allowing your environment to add to your stress and take you out of flow!"

I'm sure that you have been in this situation too. Maybe you're struggling with your mental health, so you feel unmotivated to keep your environment tidy.

Think about all the environments you move through during your normal daily routine. One by one, consider those environments and the effects they have on you mentally, physically, and emotionally. Are they inspiring you or draining you? How much do they add to your mental chaos? If our environments combine to affect us mentally, emotionally, and physically, how much of a priority should we make it to level them up?

Meet "Soccer Stan"

I have a client in Major League Soccer who was losing his flow in specific scenarios—not having his greatest games. I'll call him Stan to protect his privacy. Stan said, "Coach Dar, whenever I go to Miami, I don't play well. Thinking about it, I get anxious before leaving for the city. Nothing feels right, and it always affects my performance. I don't even like the smell of the hotel I stay in."

Miami is a place—it's an environment. So I told him, "When you go to Miami, you've got to be intentional about your environment while you're there. When you land, I want you to listen to Will Smith's 'Welcome to Miami.' I want you to eat your favorite food before the game, something healthy that makes you feel energized and strong. I want you to dress in your nicest suit for these Miami games. What's your favorite scent? Let's put that on a cotton ball in your pocket or put on your best cologne. Let's reframe this scenario from where you are—anxious about and in Miami—to Miami being a place where they will want you on their team because of how deeply in flow you are there."

Sure enough, Stan got dressed in his best suit and put his best cologne on. We had a call to get him mentally boosted up before he left, and then as he pulled up to the stadium, he put his headphones on and listened to "Welcome to Miami." You might say, "Coach Dar, come on. You don't really think playing *a song* made this guy a better athlete."

All of it did, as he played a great game and now no longer has that anxiety about going to Miami; so maybe it really is the simplest things that make the most significant difference. The environment he was living in, both mentally and physically, was not helping him, but once we changed it all for the better, he was back in flow and could now focus on what mattered much easier. Environments matters. What and who you surround yourself with matters.

BOUNCE BACK ENVIRONMENTS MATTER

How your environment influences you doesn't just mean it's visually pleasing. In fact, when we spend a lot of time somewhere, we no longer really notice what's around us. The piles of paperwork on your work-from-home desk or the laundry spilling out of your closet seem to disappear when you stop paying attention to them for a few days, or a few weeks. That's due to a phenomenon known as habituation—sometimes called "attentional blindness."

But just because you're not consciously focusing on your surroundings doesn't mean they're not taking a toll on your mental health. For example, people who are depressed don't often have the energy to clean, organize, or open the windows to let in light and air. This creates a kind of vicious cycle, as the environment becomes another factor contributing to poor mental health.

The bottom line is that when you're facing a setback, mental chaos (the result of your environments working against your Fundamental Hardwiring) will hold you back from bouncing back and moving forward. Period.

Environments matter.

My mom understood this. Growing up without a lot of money, I was always impressed by how she created the most beautiful, welcoming environment with what she had. Not because she spent a lot, but because she cared a lot. It's what experts call a "sacred space," and we can all recall places that make us feel this way. Our entire home felt like a sacred space.

Our home was maybe 1,500 square feet, but everyone who walked inside never wanted to leave. Have you ever been to someone's house and felt that way? It's almost like the person has infused their own energy into the environment. In these places, you want to linger, to stay connected to its life-giving peace and acceptance.

While my mom did it on a shoestring budget, I always thought she could have been a Disney Imagineer. Imagine what she could do with the millions of dollars Disney spends creating the most pleasing environments for their customers.

The Imagineers of Disney understand the power of the environment better than most. You just mention the name "Disney" in front of kids (or a lot of adults, frankly), and a smile spreads across their faces.

The Disney parks were intentionally designed to create environments that bring joy and a sense of wonder and magic. From where the "big" rides are located, to in-line entertainment, to the sounds and smells, a group of engineers and innovators thought through every single detail to make Disney "the happiest place on Earth."

I have also gone into 40,000-square-foot homes to coach that felt empty and lifeless because, while they might have been aesthetically decorated, there was no personality or a sense of connection to the home and the people who lived in it.

If I were to guess, I bet we'd all say that the experience of our lives holds greater significance than an experience at a theme park. And yet a company like Disney has taken the time to create environments that we visit on a vacation with incredibly intentional design, while most of us organize our environments in which we actually *live* every single day unintentionally and by default. You can become an Imagineer of your own world, no matter how much money you have or where you live. Having a leveled-up environment has very little to do with a grand financial investment; my mom is proof of that.

The Health Factor

Researchers have been studying the impact our environments have on our mental and physical wellness for decades. Some of the findings include that insufficient levels of natural and/or artificial light in your room can catalyze stress and anxiety.[1] In addition, light that's too bright at night disrupts sleep and therefore mood. In a study of women's cortisol levels compared to their husbands', the wives with cluttered homes had higher stress and a more depressed mood.[2] Along with lowering well-being, clutter has also been linked to reduced executive functioning,[3] as well as procrastination, reduced productivity, and emotional exhaustion.[4]

One of the forerunners of this work, Esther Sternberg, cites studies done by environmental psychologist Roger Ulrich in her book, *Healing Places: The Science of Place and Well-Being*.[5] In Ulrich's studies, he compared how quickly patients healed following gallbladder surgery. Patients were assigned at random to rooms that had either a view of a grove of trees or a view of a brick wall. Ulrich's study noted that patients who were put in a room with a view of the grove consistently healed faster than those who looked out on a brick wall. His findings have been confirmed by a number of similar studies, too.

See? Environments are not just how tidy we keep our homes or cars. Think about work teams and office environments.

From studies to TED Talks, people are realizing the benefits of introducing greenery to their working spaces to increase productivity and workplace happiness. According to a 2014 study published by the University of Exeter,[6] "Research showed plants in the office significantly increased workplace satisfaction, self-reported levels of concentration, and perceived air quality. Analysis into the reasons why plants are beneficial suggests that a green office increases employees' work engagement by making them more physically, cognitively, and emotionally involved in their work."

In addition, indoor air quality can be compromised by printers that emit toner particles and toxic gases such as ozone and nitrogen dioxide, which can lead to coughing and minor throat irritation to dizziness and respiratory damage.[7] Having plants or green walls surrounding you can improve air quality by helping clean the air and producing oxygen. Biophilic walls can be noise reducers and cultivate a serene atmosphere, too. Biophilic design helps with wellness as well as productivity.[8] Think about it. We spend at least eight hours a day in an office or other confined workspace, so spend the time making your office an environment that sets you up for happiness and success.

Meet "Harry"

I was hired by a company in the Midwest and worked with the CEO we'll call Harry. When I walked into the corporate office space, it felt pretty dead. I said, "First, we've got to paint here. We've got to set up the entrance so it's inviting. We must clean out everything and create a sacred workspace for your team because they cannot get into flow in an office that feels so dead."

You see, Harry wanted me to consult for him on how to get his team to better engage during a period of growth transition. He was experiencing a big setback in his business then, and the growth period was crucial to his company's survival. I can't say for sure that Harry believed me that a new coat of paint and some plants would be the way to get his employees engaged in the growth transition, but he was desperate, and there was an urgency, so he didn't argue. I went back to his office a month later and noticed he had painted the entire office a bright white with vibrant yellows.

Plants were everywhere. The brightly colored walls and plants energized and relaxed you simultaneously. A beautiful mantle with scented candles had been set up in the lobby. A tray of cookies was on a table toward the back of the room, drawing you in. The cookies and candles made the room smell good. And who doesn't love a chocolate chip cookie? Harry brought real life to his lobby area.

After taking in the new office, I asked, "Harry, how's business?"

Harry said one of the most significant gains from my coaching was the attitude of the staff showing up every day. It was booming. Morale was high, and people were on time and completing their jobs more effectively and efficiently. The hyper-focus on creating a Bounce Back Environment helped their office tremendously.

Now can you see why being intentional about our environments is an essential step in the Bounce Back coaching system?

Clutter = Chaos

Psychology Today[9] has noted that clutter leads to lower subjective well-being, unhealthy eating habits, poorer mental hygiene, less efficient visual processing, and less efficient thinking.[10]

All of that clutter that haunts your daily life isn't just troubling in your physical space; it's creating mental mess and frustration that seeps into your relationships and work style. Take time to clean that desk, clear out that car, and start making your bed in the morning! Addressing the chaos in your personal areas and creating a routine where you make time for tidiness will open your mental capacity and allow you to easily access your flow state.

BOUNCING BACK USING YOUR FIVE SENSES

While I might have you convinced that you need to do some serious cleaning, organizing, and revamping of your environment, I have to tell you something first: do not try to make significant changes in your environments without breaking things down to the level of your core perceptions—the five senses. Why? Because your five senses help you experience your environment.

In previous chapters, I talked about the importance of awareness and mindfulness when trying to get back into flow states. A simple mindfulness exercise you can practice when it comes to your environment is to notice what you are experiencing right now through any or all of your five senses: sound, sight, touch, taste, and smell. For example, simply listening to birds chirping or smelling fresh-cut grass could help you focus less on your anxious thoughts in the present moment.

Let's break down how we can be more intentional with each of the five senses together now. (See Figure 5.1.)

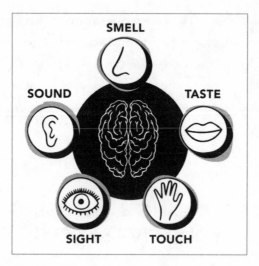

FIGURE 5.1. Practice mindfulness to assess the state of your environment and your current experience through any or all of your five senses: sound, sight, touch, taste, and smell.

The Power of Sight

What you see around you can significantly impact your mental health and performance, and be a trigger for activating your flow states. For this reason, you should make your environment peaceful and pleasing to look at. Add photos, motivational sayings, and pieces of art around you that inspire and lift you up. It matters.

One suggestion I always give my clients is to keep at least one thing in their workspace that brings them joy whenever they look at it. Maybe it's a family photo. Perhaps it's an award for a degree you've earned. Anything that brings you joy. And remember, this is in addition to your Mission Statement and Power Word, which should be written somewhere you see often.

Ask yourself the following question about what you see in your environment—and adjust accordingly:

- What in my workspace brings me joy? If the answer is "nothing," change that today.

The Power of Sound

You cannot expect to only see calming things and boost your mental health. You may feel stressed, anxious, or depressed if you hear loud and obnoxious noises, too. Therefore, filling your surroundings with good music or even a podcast can give you the sense of tranquility you are searching for. Whether you use headphones or a speaker, you are bound to enjoy the benefits.

In 2014, a group of researchers, including Dennis Hsu of Kellogg School of Management at Northwestern University, studied how music can make us feel powerful. "When watching major sports events," Hsu writes, "my coauthors and I frequently noticed athletes with their earphones on while entering the stadium and in the locker room. The way these athletes immerse themselves in the music—some with their eyes steely shut and some gently nodding along with the beats—seems as if the music is mentally preparing and toughening them up for the competition about to occur."

Hsu and his colleagues set out to find whether or not their initial observations were accurate: Can music "truly transform the psychological state of the listener"? Thirty-one pieces of music from genres like hip-hop, reggae, and "sports" music like Queen's "We Will Rock You" and 2 Unlimited's "Get Ready for This" were played in 30-second clips to see how powerful they made a listener feel. The results? "[T]he researchers found that the high-power music not only evoked a sense of power unconsciously, but also systematically generated the three downstream consequences of power."[11]

Growing up in my house, I listened to great music from Aretha Franklin to Frank Sinatra to Pavarotti to the Bee Gees to Diana Ross to Michael Jackson and Elton John. The soundtrack of my childhood is full of soul. Decades later, when I hear this music, I'm flooded with feelings of nostalgia. It's a warm, peaceful feeling. My childhood was not perfect—not by a long shot. But I knew how to make my auditory environment feel good and safe no matter the adversity around me.

Before I go to give a speech, I need to find the energy to open up or close out a conference filled with thousands of people. In those moments, you'll find me listening to Eminem, another hip-hop artist, or a movie score.

Another great way to level up your environment with sound is to set an alarm each night that plays a song on something other than your phone. Pick a song that will make you feel great when it goes off. Think of it as your walk-out song. Players come out of the tunnel or onto the field or ice to great music, so I advise all my clients to wake up to their walk-out song. I do this every morning and it's a game changer. You can start your day off with an annoying sound or an uplifting one, you choose. I can say with certainty that the latter will help you reach your flow a lot better.

We miss a huge opportunity when we fail to level up our auditory environment. I challenge you to think through the sounds of your environments. Whether you drive into work with your bass vibrating or you play an overture during your lunch break, leverage the mind's deep connection to music and sound to level up your environment and your sense of power.

Ask yourself the following questions about what you *hear* in your environment—and adjust accordingly:

- What sounds lift me up?
- What sounds help me focus?
- What songs make me feel good or bad?
- What can I be playing or noise canceling out when I work?

The Power of Smell

One environmental level-up that is often overlooked is how things smell. Like music, scientists believe that smell and memory are intrinsically connected.[12] According to Theresa L. White, PhD, people often say that the sense of smell conjures up memories so well that they feel as if they were experiencing them again. Smelling Grandma's chocolate chip cookies makes them feel as if they were back in her home.

I bet we can all think of a smell that reminds us of our childhood. For me, it's the smell of homemade sauce because every Sunday my family would make a big pasta meal and then we would watch sports together. In the same way, I can also smell my mom's perfume or my dad's cologne and feel like they are right here with me.

Researchers believe our memories become deeply connected to odors because the anatomy of the brain allows "olfactory signals to get to the limbic system very quickly."[13] The limbic system structures, such as the amygdala and hippocampus, are involved in regulating emotion and emotional memories.

Researchers from the University of California–Irvine discovered "specific types of neurons within the memory center of the brain that are responsible for acquiring new associative memories, that is, memories triggered by unrelated items, such as an odor."[14]

So if your mom used to wear musk-scented perfume, you probably associate the scent with comfort, warmth, and security. When I am missing my mom, I smell her perfume and it brings me peace. Smell has such a powerful way of helping us feel better. Find what smells and scents help you get into your state of flow and surround yourself with them. Pay attention to how the smells around you either help or hinder work, productivity, relaxation, or inspiration.

Ask yourself the following questions about what you *smell* in your environment—and adjust accordingly:

- What are the smells around you at home, in your office, or in your car?
- Do they lift you up or do they distract you?

The Power of Taste

Having something pleasing to taste can also bring you pleasure and peace of mind. This does not mean you have to constantly eat your favorite foods. Instead, you can choose a flavor of gum or mints that brings you happiness. You can also keep a bottle of your favorite drink with you, such as flavored water, tea, or coffee.

One seemingly random habit I have is chewing cinnamon gum. My friends and family all know how much I love it and will say, "Are you chewing cinnamon gum again?" Even when I played field hockey, I chewed gum with my mouth guard in. And there's probably some pretty unflattering photos of that.

Why did this work for me? Well, apparently chewing gum helps with memory and concentration by supplying your brain with more blood and increasing the amount of oxygen in your cells.[15] Maybe crunching on ice helps you stay at your desk longer and facilitates more productivity. Or eating frozen grapes. Or sipping lemon water or warm tea. This is one assessment that none of my clients mind doing. Determine what tastes keep you in a state of flow longer. And whatever it is, don't run out of it.

> **Ask yourself the following question about what you *taste* in your environment—and adjust accordingly:**
>
> - What have I chewed on or eaten that has helped me focus better or lifted me up? Is there a certain drink, gum, mint, ice chip, food?

The Power of Touch

For number five on this list, we'll talk about touch, which boosts your mental health. Humans have lived in social groups now for hundreds of thousands of years. And so we're extraordinarily good at reading other people's facial expressions, tone of voice, and body language. We're extremely well-adapted for that. But when we communicate via email, text, or on social media, all of those unspoken signals are impoverished. It's the difference between sending a sad emoji versus actually reaching out and touching someone to console them. It's the difference between hugging someone and just texting them that you are thinking of them.

Your brain releases a hormone called oxytocin when you engage in pleasant touch, like a hug. You feel good. Social research confirms touch as a positive force in creating success in various aspects of our lives:

- Newborns who are given nurturing touch grow faster and have more improved mental and motor skill development.
- Children with more physical interaction tend to be less aggressive and violent.
- Partners who cuddle are shown to have lower stress levels and blood pressure.
- Older adults who receive affirming touch have been shown to better handle the process of aging.

From the moment we are born to the final days of our lives, touch acts as a central aspect of the human experience— impacting our physical, mental, and emotional health while also shaping how we go through our lives. And, here is the exciting part. Renowned neuroscientist David Linden's book *Touch: The Science of Hand, Heart, and Mind* explores how our sense of touch, and our emotional responses genuinely impact our lives. He references a study conducted at Berkeley on professional NBA teams. The researchers scored all the celebratory touch points by reviewing every single video of every single game that NBA teams played for the first half of the season. Touch points included fist bumps, chest bumps, high fives, and taps on the rear end. Then the researchers asked: "Did that number predict anything about what would happen in the second half?" You might be surprised to learn that it did! The teams with more celebratory touches in the first half of the season won more games in the second half.

When I was traveling with the Phoenix Suns, I would be in the treatment/physical therapy room that the guys would have to walk through to get to the locker room after practice. I would give hugs and fist pumps to the guys who walked by me. I did this because I know the science behind hugs, plus you feel better when someone acknowledges you. Hugs help with mental health and your mental edge because you feel seen and safe, which gives you mental strength.

All of that being said, there are people who do not feel comfortable when being touched by others, so be respectful of that. And if you fall into that group, remember that your sense of touch does not always have to be human touch. You can wrap yourself in a warm blanket, lay outside and feel the sun on your skin, or embrace an animal.

For me when I have to write a new speech, I get into comfortable clothes and sit in my living room with a comfy blanket. Being comfortable makes me feel free to create and flow. No matter what kind of touch brings you happiness, try to seek it out to manage your mental chaos.

> **Ask yourself the following questions about what you *feel* in your environment—and adjust accordingly:**
>
> - What kind of clothing do you like to wear to feel comfortable?
> - What kind of clothing makes you feel confident?
> - What textures feel good or not to you?
> - Do you like hugs or high fives?
> - What kind of sensory input helps you flow better and what doesn't?

● ● ●

Creating an environment that supports your Fundamental Hardwiring is crucial to find your flow and set you up for raising the bar. So be sure that your environment is always supporting the life you want—whether that's the people you surround yourself, the space where you work, or the place where you live. Each plays a crucial role in your success, so be sure to create an environment for yourself that helps you thrive.

ACTIVATING EMOTIONAL INTELLIGENCE

Happiness depends upon ourselves.

—Aristotle

There's a Disney Pixar movie called *Inside Out* that I wish we could all watch together. Leave it to a kids' movie to have more profound contributions to society than modern culture.

The storyline centers around 11-year-old Riley Andersen and her five personified emotions: Disgust, Anger, Fear, Sadness, and Joy. Fresh off a move from Minnesota to San Francisco, Riley's world is in flux. She's off her game and out of her flow state. It's worth mentioning that even though she's a preteen, Riley's reaction to change is a lot like ours as adults—she flounders, vacillating from anger, to sadness, to fear, to joy, to disgust, and back again.

Along with the help of her five emotions, Riley is left to navigate a situation she didn't want and couldn't control. What's most meaningful to me about the movie's illustrations of Riley's emotions is the irreplaceable role they all play in her story and overall mental health. Though Joy tries as hard as she can to keep Sadness from rearing her whiny head, it's only through experiencing Sadness that Riley can process life and all of its transitions—and feel joy as a result! It is the same with Anger, Disgust, and Fear. Each plays a crucial role in bringing Riley toward emotional health.

An emotionally intelligent person isn't someone who is constantly positive or happy. An emotionally intelligent person is someone who understands their own emotions and how those emotions affect them and the people around them. An emotionally healthy person knows that it's OK not to be OK but also knows that being not OK isn't an excuse to be a jerk or make life hard for someone else.

With my clients, we often have to work through the lie that acknowledging and expressing your emotions will make you ineffective, weak, or disrespected. The truth is, you will be more robust and influential in any role if you can acknowledge and handle your emotions effectively. Becoming emotionally intelligent helps you bounce back from setbacks because your reactions originate in self-awareness with a focus on regulation and response.

By the end of this chapter, you will have clear skill sets for increasing your Emotional Intelligence through Agility, Neutrality, and Accountability. By being emotionally aware, you raise the bar on your own behavior and inspire others around you to do the same. Whether that's bouncing back from a slipup and not letting it derail your whole routine, remaining calm in the face of frustration, or owning up to your own shortcomings in order to improve, Emotional Intelligence is one of the most important skills you can have in your mental toolkit. It keeps you in a constant state of managing your emotional inventory to boost positive and productive engagements with others!

Taking Mental Health Issues Seriously

You have to be emotionally ready for life because it's coming on its own terms, whether you like it or not. Life doesn't care if you don't get adequate sleep. It doesn't care if you're feeling off your game. It doesn't care if you're reeling from divorce, bankruptcy, or illness. Life is nondiscriminatory. It comes for us all, and we've got to be prepared.

As a general disclaimer, we'll be talking about our emotions and our Emotional Intelligence throughout this chapter. I want to say up front that if you are someone who is suffering from medical mood disorders like bipolar disorder, manic depression, or another diagnosis of clinical depression, it's important that you work with a medical professional to get the proper care that you need. That being said, if you are reading this book, I want you to know this isn't "just choose joy," "come on, cheer up," or "turn that frown upside down" content. In fact, it's the opposite. I want this book to be the momentum you need to begin to track and understand your emotions just like we track our finances (or how we *should* track and understand our finances). And when we notice that our emotions are creating relational deficits through our negative habits and behaviors, this chapter will deliver the tools you need to adjust your emotions accordingly.

SO WHAT *IS* EMOTIONAL INTELLIGENCE?

In 1990, Peter Salavoy and John Mayer coined the term Emotional Intelligence (EQ) in an article in the journal *Imagination, Cognition, and Personality.* Five years later, Dan Goleman made the term popular thanks to his book titled *Emotional Intelligence.*[1]

In practical terms, EQ means being aware of the fact that emotions drive our behaviors. It means you can recognize and understand your emotions and those of others. EQ helps you make decisions, solve problems, and communicate more effectively. It also means that you have the social skills, self-awareness, motivation, and ability to self-reflect in order to acknowledge, understand, regulate, and reframe using emotions.

EQ is becoming incredibly important and increasingly acknowledged in the business world now, too. Intelligence and emotions have been considered opposites historically. In fact, you may have even received the long-standing advice that urges professionals to leave emotions at the door when they arrive at work. The problem with this is it doesn't acknowledge the fact that people *are* emotional. This is exactly why the interlocking of emotions and work has become a joint area of interest recently. When professionals cannot understand and handle their emotions, business problems are created. Which leads me to the answer to an important question . . .

Why Is EQ Important?

Each day, you must make decisions, most of which are influenced by your emotions. If you have a high EQ, you can understand the emotions of others, manage, and communicate your own, and solve problems efficiently. On the other hand, when there is low EQ, specifically in the workplace, people tend not to take responsibility for mistakes and not be in control of their emotions. It's harder for people to work together as a team.

When communicating, people with low EQs are either passive or aggressive, not assertive. Another noticeable characteristic of weak EQ at work is an inability to accept constructive criticism. However, those with high EQ tend to solve problems better and make suitable decisions. They also tend to keep a level head under pressure, display greater empathy, and are able to listen, reflect, and react appropriately to the opinions of others.

One of the biggest lessons I learned about EQ is that it is not singular. EQ has several sides to it that you should be consciously aware of in order to have the highest EQ in any situation. Several foundational skills of EQ are essential to understand for better performance in the workplace. (See Figure 6.1.) The more built-up these skills are, the higher your emotional intelligence.

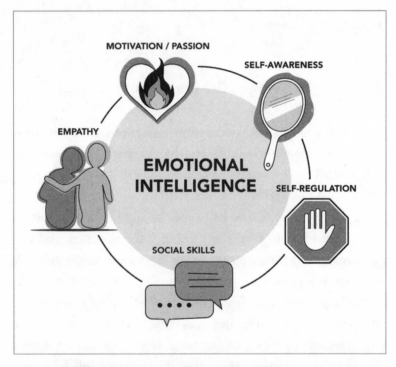

FIGURE 6.1. Five foundational skills of EQ are essential for better performance in the workplace. The more you practice these skills and take inventory of your progress with them, the greater your growth in EQ will be.

Let's dive deeper into each:

1. **Self-awareness** allows you to identify your emotions and the reactions they create. When you need to bounce back from a setback, being self-aware and knowing your emotional triggers and how they get set off is critical. The higher your EQ in this area, the better you will be able to recognize your emotional reactions as soon as they happen and bring them to a neutral place. With self-awareness, you know your strengths, weaknesses, and values, and the impressions you have on others. When you have self-awareness, you may appear more confident and receptive to constructive criticism.

2. **Self-regulation** is about understanding how you are feeling in a particular moment, choosing how to react, and ensuring you remain in a "move forward" mindset. While negative emotions like anger or fear are normal to experience during a setback, self-regulation helps you limit how long you allow yourself to feel these emotions. Practicing self-regulation can be done with exercises like meditation or my favorite technique—deep-breathing exercises. When you can put self-regulation into practice, you display an ability to redirect disruptive moods and impulses. For example, in business, when things don't turn out as you would like or your team makes a mistake, the urge might be to scold yourself or the team because of the failure. However, with EQ and self-regulation, you can see the error objectively and

look at all the causes. Then you can adjust accordingly and make sure your team understands the consequences, you can consider alternative resolutions with them, and you can ensure everyone stays in that move-forward mindset.

3. **Motivation** is often considered separate from EQ but it is quite directly connected. When you feel negative emotions during disappointing situations or big setbacks, it can be hard to see the good in the situation, much less find outside motivation to push through. An emotionally intelligent person creates their own internal motivation by setting concrete goals. When you are consciously aware of your motivation levels, it's easier to take action on your goals so you can pull yourself out of a setback.

4. **Empathy** shows up when you put yourself in other people's shoes and try to see things from their perspective. The more empathy you develop, the more open-minded you are to options, alternatives, and solutions, which all help in times of high emotions, stress, or adversity. Empathy also helps build relationships, and in times of crisis, this can be a lifesaver. Empathy plays a role in the workplace when you are sensitive to cross-cultural differences and help other people develop professionally when they might be struggling.

5. **Social skills** are important when it comes to EQ and the main requirement is to listen more than you speak. While not everyone may be comfortable in social interactions, if you practice active listening when communicating, you show others that you

are willing to treat others the way you expect to be treated, and in turn you build trust. By listening to the meanings and emotions behind the words of others, and then responding with sensitivity, honesty, and patience, you are practicing EQ through your social skills.

With consistent awareness of these five skills (and putting them into action), we activate EQ at stronger and stronger levels with each bounce back or plateau.

THE THREE BUILDING BLOCKS OF EQ

In the bestselling book *Atomic Habits*, author James Clear makes a very simple point: when successful people fail, they bounce back faster. He is absolutely correct and once you understand this fact—and I mean really get it—you become a better person, professional, teammate, partner, and leader—and definitely bounce back faster.

Why? Because you will have the emotional tools to do so! People tend to see EQ as a "soft skill" that's often overlooked, but that couldn't be further from the truth. EQ is incredibly hard because it's self-awareness in real time all the time, which takes practice every day. In addition to being aware of the five foundational skills of EQ, actually activating and practicing EQ requires building and strengthening three specific mental skills through awareness: Emotional Agility, Emotional Neutrality, and Emotional Accountability.

Combined, these three skills will boost your overall EQ, so let's learn more about each in depth and understand how we can practice these building blocks in our day-to-day lives!

Building Block 1 of EQ: Emotional Agility

Whenever you think of a palm tree, you probably imagine sunshine and a sandy shore, but that's not always the reality. Those tropical shorelines where palm trees thrive are subject to hurricane-intensity winds and rains for entire seasons! And yet palm trees remain resilient. They don't snap or break like their inland counterparts when they meet a massive storm.

How? Palm trees are very elastic. They have big fibrous trunks that contain a lot of moisture, which allows them to bend almost down to the ground without snapping, then come back up when the strong winds pass. They don't just remain to stand; they thrive in this environment where other trees can't. They grow, they multiply, and they can teach us a lesson in emotional agility.

When it comes to the destructive winds of adversity that life sweeps across our path, we've got to be able to bend like the palm tree instead of snapping in half like a birch and crushing a nearby house. With acceptance and determination, we've got to go in the direction of the wind for a time and then bounce back when the hurricane is past us. If we're too rigid, if we reject or refuse, we'll snap, and that can hurt both us and those around us.

After my stroke, I spent a few weeks wallowing. I was rigid. I didn't accept the reality that I was being given. But *I knew* that I could either let fear eat away at the time that I had left, or I could bounce back to live the fullest life possible. I was determined to remain emotionally agile, process my negative emotions, learn from them, and appreciate every minute I have in order to help others live life to the fullest and reach their maximum potential before it's too late.

The practice of emotional agility focuses on remaining flexible in order to take on the pressure of strong winds in our lives and bend with them instead of snapping and stopping any chance of progression.

Practicing Emotional Agility

When it comes to life, triggers and disappointments are bound to happen, even in places where you least expect them. The account that you thought was going to close doesn't. The supplies you've been waiting for finally show up, and they're wrong. You think you'll start the game, but the coach changes the lineup at the last minute. The client you've specifically designed a presentation for doesn't show up, and now you've got to figure out how to calm your emotions and decide what you are going to do.

Practicing Emotional Agility and keeping your emotions in check in any of these situations would be a challenge, but it's necessary.

I coach a young man who is training for the Olympics in gymnastics. We've been working on his Emotional Agility—even in the middle of a routine. When you're whipping around a wooden bar at warp speed, one slip of a pinkie finger could send you face-first into a mat. There's zero room for error.

This client recently competed and made a small mistake on the pommel horse, but because he's built up his Emotional Agility over time, he was able to recover quickly and not let his emotions alter the rest of his routine. He didn't let that mistake send him into a spiral about his shortcomings. Instead, he remained agile and finished his routine with precision and earned a place on the podium.

The human mind can organize our emotions and reassign their significance to allow us to perform unaffectedly in the moments that matter most. But this is a skill that takes time, discipline, and effort. By focusing on Emotional Agility, you too can manage your emotions in real time and handle a trigger or disappointment with a new, productive angle instead of spiraling and allowing one slipup to continue disrupting your routine.

Remember: Emotional agility comes with practice. It's like a muscle that you work over and over again. You need to develop it, adding more emotional weight over time in order to grow your overall self-awareness and, in turn, EQ. Is it fun? Not really. It can be incredibly uncomfortable and exhausting to acknowledge your emotions and feelings at any given moment—but it's necessary.

Exercise: Take Daily Inventory

It's vital to archive your thoughts so you can start to see patterns to improve your Emotional Agility over time. One way to do this is through journaling. And don't worry, if traditional journaling is difficult for you, we live in a world where technology is at our fingertips, making *digital* journaling an inviting alternative.

One way to do this is create daily video journals or audio logs. Simply record videos or voice notes as a way into your successes, barriers, and breakthroughs, making you better at real-time reflection and pivots in the moment.

Every day, ask yourself:

- What were my emotional/mental skill wins today?
- What were the places where my emotional/mental skills needed improvement?
- How can I improve on areas where I was struggling?

We *need* reflection. We *need* to take inventory. And where we see we could have done something better, we need to be honest about it. Sometimes that might require us to call someone and apologize. Or to scale back plans, pivot, and shift.

Without self-reflection, the only guarantee is that we will eventually get off course.

Building Block 2 of EQ: Emotional Neutrality

Trevor Moawad was the cofounder of Limitless Minds and a sports psychologist who worked with professional athletes like pitcher Marcus Stroman and quarterback Russell Wilson, as well as the football programs of Alabama, Florida

State, and Georgia before succumbing to cancer in late 2021. As part of an immeasurably impactful legacy, Moawad coined the term "neutral thinking." Neutral thinking is the idea that a person can receive information without assigning positive or negative emotions to it.

About a year before his passing, Moawad was on Tom Bilyeu's podcast "Impact Theory" and this is how he explained the power of neutral thinking: "I started thinking about a car. A car going backward can't automatically go forward, so it has to shift into neutral, and then it stops. At that point, you can either go forward by changing your behavior, or you can go backward by doing the same stupid shit you were doing."

Moawad said that the words we say in situations of high pressure (or high emotion) tend to steer the direction of our actions and reactions and how the result is often the opposite of what we want it to be. Think about it. If you've ever been pissed off in a meeting and let your emotions take control while you lashed out, you probably walked away feeling a little embarrassed or guilty. At the very least, you wished you would have handled it better.

Emotional Neutrality works the same way. Emotional Neutrality acknowledges the emotions of the moment, but before you decide what to do with those emotions, you put your emotions into neutral, just like that car. You're not positive. You're not negative.

When you practice Emotional Neutrality, you remain still as you process the inputs of information surrounding the situation.

Practicing Emotional Neutrality

Our brains bounce back best when we train them to remain calm in difficult situations instead of falling into fight-or-flight mode. Imagine a Newton's Cradle (that device you see on people's desks in movies, with metal balls that clink). When you're triggered and responding emotionally, you become that first ball to move, sending a shock wave through your team and possibly triggering someone else to fly off the handle on the opposite side of you. (See Figure 6.2.) Emotional Neutrality is the practice of stillness, of slowing the shock waves until everyone is back at center and sitting in harmony with one another.

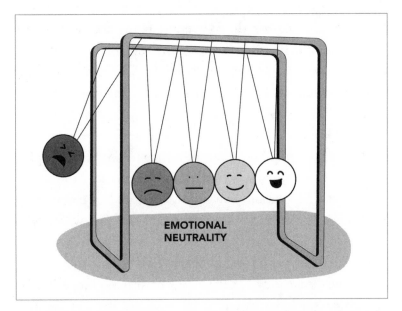

EMOTIONAL
NEUTRALITY

FIGURE 6.2. When you are able to assess the highs and lows of your emotional reactions, process them, and respond logically to a situation, you avoid sending a shock wave through your team that puts everyone in a triggered and disrupted state.

I was recently coaching a C-level executive—we'll call Rob—and trying to work with him to rein in the reactive problems he was having. Rob had a brilliant business mind but struggled with shortsightedness. One might say that he often found himself having significant interpersonal conflicts from seemingly minor issues, making mountains out of molehills.

Whenever a problem happened, I'd get a panicked call declaring an executive state of emergency! The alarms were going off!

"They've done me wrong again, Dar," he would say. "My team is out to get me; they want to see me fail."

I noticed right away that Rob was caught up in his emotions from a tense situation. He felt frustrated, maybe even embarrassed, because things weren't going the way he was hoping, and he might look foolish by someone else's design. The paranoia was settling in, fueled by his fears. Logic was out the window at that moment, but I knew I could get it back.

"Your emotions are in control of this situation," I explained to him. "You're not in control, and this is keeping you from processing the information that you need to actually work toward a solution. You've got to get into an emotionally neutral gear so we can talk about what's true and what's false before you communicate with your team. Take a few deep breaths, and let's run through what you're saying to me."

As we broke down the facts of the situation together, he started to see how his emotions were playing a major role in his reactions and was able to move past the barrier of how information was making him *feel*. Once he saw everything clearly and understood why he had the reaction he did, he was finally able to move forward and communicate a solution.

When Rob took time to change his state, pull himself out of his volatile emotions, and return to the situation with stability, he would make great decisions—*really excellent ones*!

● ● ●

If you find yourself in a state like Rob did, where your emotions take over and you feel you've lost control of them, ask yourself the following self-reflection questions:

- **What could have been done differently?**
- **What is the game plan for the next time you feel devalued?**
- **How can you process mistakes and conflicts without slipping into victim mode and paranoia again?**
- **Is what I'm feeling true or false? Are my emotions leading rather than the facts?**
- **Am I being triggered by an old wound that is not relevant to the current situation?**

Not only will these questions help you find a solution for the situation at hand, they will also set you up for success in the future because you'll see what went wrong this time and be able to apply it earlier next time—well before those emotions take control of the wheel. Another way to help you practice Emotional Neutrality is to know and understand your emotional triggers and your response to them.

Take five minutes now to ruminate on what triggers you. What are the things, moments, things people say, or situations that stop you in your tracks? How do you typically respond to each of these triggers? Anxiety? Anger? Tears? Once you have them all laid out, it will be much easier for you to be more aware when those situations arise, so you can manage your emotions accordingly.

In the military, they say, "Embrace the suck." If you're finding yourself in an emotional moment with a trigger that you maybe hadn't prepared to face or an unexpected disappointment that's really throwing you off your game, remember to change your state and have a little check-in. You've got to embrace the suck of allowing yourself to feel and, at the same time, not have a knee-jerk reaction to those feelings. You're simply being still and gaining awareness before continuing.

The process can look as simple as:

1. Accept the emotion or situation by mentally dropping into neutral, choosing to pause before you respond.
2. Name exactly what you're feeling. Anger? Rejection? Sadness? Overwhelmed?
3. Practice breathing, prayer, or meditation to address the physical symptoms of the emotion.
4. Name what you're feeling.
5. Own your part in the situation.
6. Ask, "What is the best way to process and address, and if anything, what am I going to do about the way I feel?"

Every time we work through our emotions, we get better and better at it. We're able to work through tense situations without flying off the wall or breaking down. We train our brains to get more emotionally agile, allowing us to bounce back from previously devastating emotional experiences.

When something good happens, it happens. When something bad happens, it happens. Most of the time, the best course of action is to acknowledge, accept, process, learn, adjust, release, and move on. Move on toward a course of action—or just move on. We can learn to release negative emotions by switching gears to neutral; it frees our minds and hearts to move toward positivity or to think better and make effective decisions.

Exercise: Snap Out of It

To practice Emotional Neutrality and snap out of negative emotions, you may need to change up your situation. Some ways you can do this include:

1. Put on or interact with a comforting scent to ground you.
2. Practice brief mindfulness/breathing to get back to the center.
3. Take a walk and get moving to break up the routine. If you can go outside and get some fresh air, all the better!
4. Make a call to a loved one and ask and talk through emotions in a safe space.
5. Watch or listen to something that will bring you out of your current emotions: comedy or uplifting

videos with funny animals can be a great resource to get you laughing and away from the immediate feelings of negativity!

Building Block 3 of EQ: Emotional Accountability

Accountability isn't easy, and constructive criticism can be hard to swallow, but there are serious consequences when you can't own up to your struggles and mistakes and then take control of your emotions to work toward success.

Emotional Accountability helps you bounce back faster from adversity and push though limiting plateaus by setting up an internal feedback loop and inventory of your mental well-being so you can act proactively instead of reactively.

Practicing Emotional Accountability

Have you ever worked for or with someone who was emotionally unpredictable? When there's a catalytic event, you don't know what they're going to do. They could stonewall you, blow up at you, shut down and give you the silent treatment, or yell and bang their fists as they blame you for what went wrong. It's like navigating a minefield with someone who lacks Emotional Accountability.

When you take Emotional Accountability for your actions, you admit when your emotions got the best of you in any situation. For example, let's say your boss walked up to you one day and said, "You're seriously underperforming recently and if you don't turn things around, I'll have to let you go." If you were to yell and run away and cry, but later come back and apologize to your boss for that reaction, you would be practicing Emotional Accountability.

Being emotionally accountable plays a major role in EQ and without it, those around you may not feel safe, you may not be considered for certain roles, and you may not find the success you would have if you had been able to take responsibility and admit you could have reacted differently.

If you find yourself in a situation where you know you could have responded differently emotionally, ask yourself the following self-reflective questions:

- How could I have reacted differently?
- Whom do I need to speak with and potentially apologize to because I let my emotions get the best of me in the moment?
- What will I do next time to make sure I don't have to take Emotional Accountability for my actions?

Exercise: Holding Yourself Accountable

As you practice Emotional Accountability, you will struggle along the way. Whenever that happens, take the time to work through this series of questions that will help you hold yourself accountable to yourself and the people around you:

Listening Up
- Am I listening to others well?
- Am I listening to myself well?

Loving Up

- Am I loving others well?
- Am I loving myself well?

Leading Up

- Am I leading others well?
- Am I leading myself well?

Leveling Up

- Am I leveling up others well?
- Am I leveling up myself well?

• • •

In the end are my actions ones I would be proud of if I watched them back on film? If not, change them. We all must hold ourselves to a high level of accountability in order to reach our greatest levels in life.

Everyone sees EQ as a soft skill, but soft skills are hard. EQ allows you as a leader to be in control of yourself; it will enable you to respond, not react, leading to more success and better team unity. Having a handle on your emotions is a huge part of finding your flow state and bouncing back.

Let's face it, taking the time to build up all areas of your EQ is hard work, but it makes it easier for you to be adaptable, resilient, and emotionally ready for anything. Now that you are aware of the building blocks of EQ (Agility, Accountability, and Neutrality), finding ways to strengthen your EQ on a daily basis will become much easier—and worth the results!

REFRAMING SETBACKS

A reframe is not about telling yourself that your fear is wrong. Reframes are about finding another way to look at the possibilities of your life.

–Rebecca K. Sampson,
author of *Stronger Now: How to Thrive in Any Circumstance and Become Unstoppable*

When I had my strokes, especially the most recent one, I would quickly fall into post-stroke depression, an often overlooked and unaddressed issue caused by vascular restriction. While fighting through recovery to get my strength back. I was covered in fear, frustration, uncertainty, and the micro-perspective of the whole experience. There were days when I couldn't get out of bed, not because I was physically unable, but because my mindset was stuck in self-pity, sadness, and a lack of hope. Even when you have a solid idea of who you are, how you get into flow best, and how to articulate your purpose, it can still be hard to see the way forward when adversity hits.

Adversity is a part of life. There are going to be times you will feel defeat, sadness, grief, and loss. You'll also have days where the worst-case scenario is playing in your mind on repeat. And while all of those feelings may be real, in order to actually move forward, you have to reframe the situation.

Mental reframing is the process by which such situations or thoughts are challenged and changed. Reframing is how you talk to yourself about the setbacks you are facing; it's about innovating the setback with a positive framework.

Finally, one day while lying in bed, I thought, *Dar, you've got to think bigger if you're going to bounce back from this.*

To think bigger and make a plan to bounce back, I had to reframe the situation so my mindset would flip the victim script that was stuck in my head.

So I got myself together and a few weeks later I went to give a keynote speech with impaired balance and the inability to fully speak consistently. I was struggling with expressive aphasia, which is when you know what you want to say but the wrong word comes out. Despite that, I was going to give a keynote. Why? Because as an occupational therapist, I knew that I needed to get right back into my daily routine and familiar flow. And guess what? It worked and I was able to give the speech—impairments and all.

What I did was reframe the game and thought, *What's the worst that can happen? You're giving a speech, not doing brain surgery.* And with that, I had the mental weight of it removed, which let me flow.

There is a light at the end of the recovery tunnel; I still have my mind and my mobility—which many people lose to major strokes. I am still able to help people, which is my purpose. By reframing my situation, I could make a plan forward—and so can you! I discovered an inner fire that no person or experience could completely extinguish.

REFRAMING AN NHL TEAM

I got a call from an NHL team to work with them during the Covid lockdown. The team was feeling out of flow and didn't believe things would improve. They were mentally worn down and physically worn out. Playoff season was on their horizon, when months' worth of bruises, injuries, and long hours on the ice took their toll on a hockey player's body and psyche. Add in the insulating factor of quarantine regulations, and you've got an implosion waiting to happen.

"Let's reframe this situation," I told the team. "Right now, people in the military are fighting for your right to play this sport in front of thousands of fans. Yeah, you may not see your family and friends for two months. But those men and women stationed overseas may not be back home for *two years*. They don't have an option right now, and you do."

We talked through the reframing process together (which I'll take you through later in this chapter). We asked and answered:

- How can the adversity of quarantine advance me?
- How can the pain of missing my family lead to purpose?
- How can the obstacles of this season become an opportunity?

I reminded them, "There are people on this planet worried about their next meal. About food and shelter. Yeah, your situation sucks, but you're also getting to do what you love. I know it's not easy and I know this is a tough situation, but there's light at the end of the tunnel, and potentially, one of the greatest things you'll ever celebrate is a run to the Stanley Cup."

While the team didn't take the Stanley Cup that season, they did advance to the playoffs. And maybe most impressive, they were able to find a way to thrive in a time when the entire world was struggling to bounce back. It just took the ability to reframe their mindsets to what they had rather than what they lacked. To what they were playing for rather than playing without.

REFRAMING YOUR OBSTACLES

Reframing does not mean you ignore the negative emotions you're feeling; it means you accept them and don't put so much weight on them. We should not deny ourselves the right to our pain, but it doesn't have to be crippling. Research shows that there are measurable health benefits to accepting negative emotions and thoughts.[1] As ironic as it sounds, studies show that people who accept their negative emotions instead of judging their negative emotions actually experience fewer negative emotions. Why? Because when you live in a state of radical acceptance, when you embrace the suck and reframe the game, you're less likely to act on emotions you define as "bad" or negative and the feelings dissipate, allowing you to bounce back faster.[2] While we may not have full power over our emotions, we do have full power over where we focus our thoughts and energy in response to our emotions—especially negative ones.

Just like you need to intentionally set up your surrounding environments so they support your Why Power and flow states so you can bounce back from disruptions, trauma, and major setbacks, you must also learn to reframe situations to reduce your emotional reactions to them.

When setbacks come our way, we must reevaluate what we are doing and see how we can improve it. This can lead to innovations that help us bounce back higher and better than before. To innovate, we need to practice the art of reframing.

Reframing says: "This sucks. But I know it's temporary. How can I learn from this experience, lean into it, and become better because of it?"

This fable by inspirational author and speaker Joyce Meyer illustrates and simplifies what it means to reframe: "There once was a woman who woke up one morning, looked in the mirror, and noticed she had only three hairs on her head. 'Well,' she said, 'I think I'll braid my hair today.' So she did, and she had a wonderful day.

"The next day, she woke up, looked in the mirror, and saw that she had only two hairs on her head. 'Hm . . . mm . . . ,' she said, 'I think I'll part my hair down the middle today.' So she did, and she had a grand day.

"The next day, she woke up, looked in the mirror, and noticed that she had only one hair on her head. 'Well,' she said, 'Today, I'm going to wear my hair in a ponytail.' So she did, and she had a fun, fun day.

"The next day she woke up, looked in the mirror, and noticed that there wasn't a single hair on her head. '*Yay!*' she exclaimed. 'I don't have to fix my hair today!'" [3]

Full disclosure, even as a mental conditioning coach, I would have trouble reframing this scenario, and yet this is the reality for so many cancer patients. They have to master this concept of reframing *while* fighting for their lives.

ACTIVE REFRAMING

To understand reframing, we have to define what a frame is. A mental frame is a lot like a physical picture frame—it's our point of reference at any given moment. It's our way of looking at a situation—our own cognitive bias. Our frames have a massive impact on the decisions we make and the words we say.

A few years after my stroke at 25, I got a divorce. We had been planning to start a family, and as that was no longer an option, we saw our lives going in different directions. I was so angry at the chain of events and how my plans for my life were no longer possible. This was a big setback. In order to overcome it, I had to reframe my circumstances.

When it comes to framing, you are presented with two different options, but both have the same outcome. When adversity does come, you get to choose how you view it—you get the opportunity to reframe something hard into a situation that you might gain something from.

Bouncing back from adversity is next to impossible without learning how to shift your perspective in the face of obstacles or roadblocks. Again, this takes intentional action and some behind-the-scenes repetition in order to become a natural part of our mental processes.

A Cup or Faces?

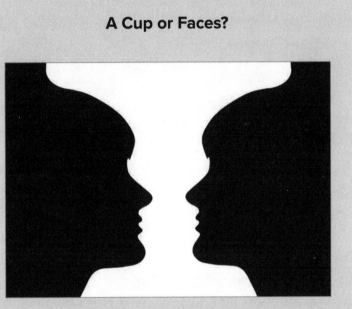

FIGURE 7.1. A cup or faces?

Figure 7.1 is a great example of a frame and reframe. The frame is whatever you see when you look at the image.

So what is it? A goblet-shaped cup (the white portion)? Or two faces mirroring each other (the black portion)?

What you see is your perception of what this picture is meant to display. Our understanding gives meaning that may or may not be accurate.

So often people go through things in life, and because of their belief system, past experiences, or disposition, they perceive reality to be a certain way. But sometimes, we're wrong. And almost every time, there's more than one way to look at any given situation. Understanding how to train our minds to reframe adversity as opportunity is how we begin to reframe the game.

RECOGNIZING THE MICRO-MOMENTS WHEN REFRAMING

Sometimes, a roadblock in our mission isn't just a hurdle to overcome but a message to shift directions.

While coaching one business leader, I found this to ring out especially true. After a day spent drafting up a thoughtful letter and preparing this fantastic client of mine to approach his boss for a well-deserved promotion, our effort was met with scorn. It was heartbreaking to watch this confident leader get stuck in a feeling of inadequacy and failure because the goal he had set forth for himself wasn't coming to fruition. He had worked hard and brought value to the company. This disappointment consumed his thoughts with disappointment, and he was ready to give up and spend his days in this job with a "Dead End" sign ever-present in the back of his mind.

"Whoa, whoa, whoa," I told him. "I know it's easy to see this as a failure, but think of ways that we can reframe this! What's better? Are you going to stay here, stuck at a dead end with a company that isn't seeing your value or letting you serve your mission statement? Or is this the message you needed to realize that there isn't a path forward here, that you don't even really *want* to be here, and now have the *opportunity to grow* past this place?"

It's like a light bulb went off for him! He was so wrapped up in the micro-moment of rejection that leaving to pursue better opportunities at a place that appreciated him more hadn't even occurred to him. I'm happy to say after that reframing, he saw a new opportunity and took it and it's been the best thing for him to date.

Focusing on setbacks and the emotions they cause is a micro way of focusing. But reframing your mindset and looking at the macro is a way to dull the sharp feelings of loss, disappointment, or anger to see what lessons and opportunities can branch off from the point you're currently at.

Micro to Macro

When you're in the middle of adversity, it can be extremely difficult to see a way out. You're experiencing that moment, that struggle, in the *micro* (microscope). You're in it, moving through it, and facing all of the emotional barriers and breakdowns that it brings. In order to gain perspective that will get you back in tune with your flow, take it to the *macro* (telescope) level.

There's power in processing our problems through writing. Science tells us that the physical act of writing something down on a sheet of paper is associated

with more "robust brain activation in multiple areas," leading to stronger neural encoding and memory retrieval.[4] In other words, we can actually change the neural pathways in our brains by writing something down. Next time you are in the middle of adversity, journal your experience as it is at the moment.
For example:

> *Experiencing a breakup is very difficult. I am feeling lonely and mourning the loss of what I thought would be a loving, healthy, and long-term commitment to another person. This adjustment is painful and constantly on my mind as I'm going through a routine without my ex.*

Then try to look at it from a bird's-eye view. Visualize a separation from your current emotional state and get the macro as it applies to your journey. Try:

> *Yes, breakups are hard at the moment, but they are a part of my journey to finding a partner to support me for the rest of my life. I still have my friends and family that are a massive part of my life; I am not alone and never will be, even as significant others come and go. This relationship ending has taught me what I need from future partners and the level of respect that I deserve in a healthy, loving relationship. A loss of a commitment that lacked stability is more beneficial for me in the long run and creates room for growth and future success.*

"HAVE TO" VERSUS "GET TO"

Author Jon Gordon talks about those two seemingly innocuous words that hold great power over our mindset: *have to.*

"So often," says Gordon, "we say things like, 'I have to take the kids to practice.' 'I have to go to this meeting.' 'I have to finish this project.' 'I have to go to work today.' 'I have to take care of this customer.' 'I have to share this new information with my team.' 'I have to see my family this weekend.' We act as if we don't have a choice. As if we are imprisoned by a paycheck and the expectations of a world that forces us to do things we don't want to do.

"But in reality, we do have a choice," Gordon writes. "We can choose our attitude and our actions. We can choose how we view our life and work. We can realize that every day is a gift. It's not about what we have to do. It's about what we get to do."[5]

Gordon points out that his mom passed away at 59 and how remembering the brevity of her life helps him reframe most problems he faces. My own mother had her first triple bypass surgery when she was 40 years old. For the next 23 years, I watched her undergo countless procedures and setbacks. But I can't remember hearing her complaining one single time.

One of the most common reframing scenarios that people go through in their lifetime is coming to terms with the loss of a loved one and figuring out how to fill the hole in your chest that loss leaves behind. My mom was an amazing woman. She could literally be 10 minutes out from having heart surgery and say, "I know if God still has me here, then I still have a purpose. I can't wait to return to the barbershop because I know the people sitting in my chair are supposed to be there for me to pour encouragement into them." My family likes to joke that by the time my mom was in her late sixties, she may not have done the best haircuts, but people didn't care because they just wanted to be with her. Hearing her encouragement or words of wisdom, receiving a loving kick in the pants—those were the things that brought people to her chair; the haircuts were an added bonus!

That was the magic she had in her heart; she just always knew how to reframe a situation to see the good, even in the middle of the pain. When her health was becoming a barrier for her, and there were days filled with tears and uncertainty, she would quickly remind herself to reframe her thinking and use it to fuel her.

She is my hero to this day; losing her was one of the most difficult experiences of my life. I wanted to be like her, to face that loss with strength and grace. It wasn't until I sat down and really thought about and committed to finding how in the world I could possibly reframe such a devastating experience that I was able to really follow in my mom's footsteps. I realized that her guiding light hadn't been extinguished but now burned in me. Instead of mourning her loss, I decided to carry her with me wherever I went and celebrate her life at every opportunity, making the most of the lessons she taught me and the joy she brought to others. It's something that I think we all do when we lose those near and dear to us, but we may not think about starting that healing process and transitioning from grief to gift.

GRATITUDE AND REFRAMING

Reframing says that instead of complaining that our lives are too hectic, we're grateful to have a home. A roof over our heads. A bed. A car. Reframing says that instead of complaining about our kids' practice schedules or school events, we're able to be grateful our kids are active and engaged. Reframing says that when business slows down, and the calls stop rolling in, we can view the downturn as an opportunity to innovate and shift our strategy to grow and stretch in new ways.

Reframing is a form of gratitude.

It's not something I have *to do*. It's what I get *to do*. As Gordan says, "We get to interact with our employees and customers and make a difference in their life. We use our gifts and talents to make a product or provide a service. We get to eat three meals daily while millions of people are starving. We get to work on projects, answer phone calls, serve customers, participate in meetings, design, create, share, sell, lead, and suit up every day for the game of life."

Viewing setbacks and adversity through this lens, it is hard to think of a situation where reframing wouldn't help you bounce back.

REFRAMING THE NEPHEW

I coached my nephew when he graduated college to help him reframe some adversity he was experiencing at work.

121

He graduated college and had a job—both positive, right? The only problem was he absolutely hated that job. It's one thing to go into a job and think, *I wonder if I'll like this* and then end up not liking it. It's a far more challenging experience when you enter a job thinking it's going to be a dream and then realizing it's not for you. That's compounded disappointment.

Part of why my nephew hates the job so much is that he's working ridiculous hours as a nurse. He worked six days a week from 4 a.m. to 7 p.m. Now he's doing shifts of 6 p.m. to 4 a.m. Is anyone immediately reframing their work hours with gratitude right now? I know I am.

My nephew said, "Auntie Dar, I have no life. I have to work at night. This is awful." I told him to hang in there. "I know this is awful," I said. "I know you don't even want to do this anymore. But you're in your first job. These are the days when you're putting in your time. There are nurses who have to work the night shift for a couple of years to get on the day shift. They have to work to get where they want to go. If you want to stay within this industry, you've got to put in the work."

My family and I helped him reframe a brutal schedule as an investment in his future. Did the hours still stink? Absolutely. But a shift in his mental perspective took him from throwing in the towel right away to sticking it out a little longer. This helped him get his head back in the game, which allowed him to find a new position at another company that he loves.

What he thought was a bad career choice was just some growing pains. Not all scenarios will be perfect, but they are not final, so don't let the bad consume you. Reframe the game and watch how much changes around you for the better. Suddenly, frustration turns to hope, and obstacles turn to opportunities.

REFRAMING THE HIGH-PERFORMANCE ATHLETE

One of my favorite examples of reframing comes from my work with a professional athlete in the NBA who had torn his ACL (anterior cruciate ligament). We talked about what it meant to be on the sidelines. It's not just benched players in those chairs. There are coaches there too. So I said, "What are you going to be? Are you going to be a player who can't play, or will you be a leader?" He was hurt. There's no getting away from that. That's the given outcome. But he got to choose how he let this affect his game.

This player worked with his team on the same mental skills we'd been practicing together. His leadership changed the entire team's chemistry and attitude. The difference was so measurable that he had an article written about him in the paper and a news outlet covered the story. This is a great story on the surface, right? But what you don't know is this same player had always struggled with speaking up. He'd never really used his voice before because his talent had always been so loud.

But he reframed his injury. He tapped into a reservoir of leadership he hadn't known existed prior to being taken out of the game. He said, "I would never have been the type of man I am today if I hadn't been hurt and working with you.

I wouldn't have known I had this within me and capacity for such influence and impact."

Ironically, he came back to the game only to get hurt again. He tore his *other* ACL. I was concerned about whether he would be able to reframe this one, but I didn't have to. He said, "Normally this would have destroyed me. This would have sunk me. But I can't view this as another setback. I have to view this as another setup." I was so proud of his ability to now reframe adversity in real time.

The young man ended up getting traded to a great team with great potential. He had the skills to process the changes; he healed a second time, bounced back, and went on to thrive the following season, make it to the playoffs, and win a division title.

I had another athlete give me a call near the end of his season in the MLB. He had been an up-and-coming player early on, and there had been a lot of buzz around his potential as an athlete. He'd started off the year incredibly well, but then he hit a slump.

This happens a lot in business, too. We come into a company or a position, and there's some chatter about our abilities. There's a level of expectation. This kind of pressure can be intense. Now we're getting paid. Now we're getting noticed. Now we have to perform. All of which can sometimes result in performance anxiety.

Nothing's changed about our ability, but we get off of our game.

This baseball player said, "Coach, I don't know what's going on with me. The pressure is unbearable."

So we got to work. How can we reframe this pressure? It's not going to go away on its own. It's something we're going to have to manage. What are the potential positives of being under a microscope? For one, pressure is a privilege; the pressure meant he was talented. He'd gotten noticed. He moved from the background of his sport to becoming a rising star. If there wasn't something special about the guy, this dynamic would have never existed. The challenge he faced was evidence of the solution—remembering that he was a great player and someone worth watching.

This baseball player came back the next season with a reframed perspective. He ended up having an epic year and he made the all-star team. He's still in the game today in a total state of flow. As I sit here writing this chapter, he *just* had a record-scoring game yesterday.

Leadership Pressure in the Workplace

If you're in an executive position or working your way in that direction and you feel an immense amount of pressure, be thankful. Let that pressure become your backbone, because pressure only finds the worthy. If you've been trusted to do a big job and it feels like everybody's watching you, that means somewhere along the line someone noticed you and your talent and trusted that you were the person to tap for that role. Tennis legend Billie Jean King said, "Pressure is a privilege."[6]

THE POWER OF PERSPECTIVE

Remember that basketball player from our third chapter where we discussed the importance of finding our flow and identifying our gifts? The star athlete who was disrupted from flow and convinced that he was no longer good at playing basketball after some rough games? Well, his story fits here too in what I like to call the power of perspective. You see, while it was extraordinarily helpful to get back to basics and understand his skills, another practice I had to show him was using perspective and introspection in order to reframe the situation.

I would say, *"Bad at basketball?* What do you mean?! You're getting so wrapped up in this negative self-talk that you've forgotten how far you've come. You are a professional athlete competing in the top 1 percent of your sport. Your skills and your position are the dream of young basketball players all over the country, if not the world! We need to find your flow again, yes, but you also need to reflect on your negative self-talk and discern fact from fiction."

In the same way that we used the three filtering questions to talk to others during the section on cultivating our environment for flow, we can use those questions as a guide for self-talk. Much like gossip can damage our social environment, negative self-talk that's formed from anxious half-truths and a lack of perspective can damage our flow and confidence. So ask yourself these three questions:

1. Is what I'm saying/thinking about myself TRUE?
2. Is what I'm saying/thinking about myself GOOD?
3. Is what I'm saying/thinking about myself USEFUL?

When you find yourself struggling to see a path forward, and you have a lack of perspective, ask yourself these questions and then use your answers to reframe your setbacks and create a plan for action!

CULTIVATING GRIT

At various points, in big ways and small, we get knocked down. If we stay down, grit loses. If we get up, grit prevails.

—Angela Duckworth,
American academic, psychologist,
and popular science author of *Grit*

Human beings are immeasurably strong. We're only as weak as our mental fortitude permits us to be. We don't push ourselves the extra hour, the extra mile, or have difficult conversations because it's easier to hide in our comfort zones. Often, we stop short of overcoming challenges and reaching our greatness because we give up too soon. Having mental and emotional grit to adapt to any situation will build an unbeatable resiliency that helps us bounce back.

One of my mentors, Mary, lived through the Holocaust. She tells stories of how she was in the middle of persecution in concentration camps and had to watch many of her aunts, uncles, and cousins die. Then World War II ended, and they were released. Her parents thought they were finally going to make it.

Then when boarding a boat to come to America, they were denied passage because of a piece of paper they didn't know they needed to have. They had to wait to get onto another boat and finally made it to America, where her dad got a job. The only place they could afford to rent was a hall-way. Not a room. A *hallway*. They would get one piece of bread to share for an entire meal. Mary got a job working at a factory as soon as she could, even though she was just a kid. Mary would grow up to become a model, but the most beautiful thing about Mary is her ability to show grit even through circumstances that would level the rest of us.

Grit has nothing to do with luck.

Grit has nothing to do with intelligence.

Grit has nothing to do with talent.

Grit has nothing to do with what we want or hope for.

Instead, grit is one's ability to tolerate hardships and keep a goal-focused mindset in order to reach the other side.

Principle 8 in the Bounce Back Coaching System is about developing the skills to cultivate grit so you can be more resilient when faced with adversity, trauma, and set-backs. I like to view grit as a skill we build over time, an endurance to match the ways adversity can test us and push us to our limits. If you experience sunshine and roses daily, you will find that one big adverse experience is enough to take the wind out of you and completely derail your life. But when you tackle adversity head-on and use obstacles as an opportunity to develop your grittiness and strengthen your resiliency muscles, you have more room to succeed when challenges do come your way.

Much like a runner whose legs are starting to feel like noodles so close to the finish line, we need to push just a little further with each challenge—at every point that we feel like checking out or throwing in the towel—and build up just a little bit more of that endurance, that's grit.

DEFINING GRIT AND ITS IMPORTANCE

It's been my experience that everyone has grit, they just may not know it yet because the opportunity to recognize and develop it hasn't come up. Grit prioritizes our thoughts and strategies, informs our decisions, and gets us through the relentless pursuit of a singular goal or ideal. It's the gas in our tank.

One of the most wonderful by-products of adversity in life and business is the development of our grit muscle. If it hadn't been for the Covid-19 crisis, I don't think I'd be writing this book. This book in itself has been a journey toward grit. I've been trying to write it since 2012 when I was first offered a book deal. After taking time off to heal from my stroke, then more time off to recoup after losing my mom, Covid struck, and that initial deal evaporated.

That would have been the period at the end of a sentence without grit. It would have signaled a story's end and the book's closing. Instead of allowing that "no" to be a period, I reframed the events to create a comma.

- This "no" doesn't mean never.
- This "no" means not yet.
- I am one "no" closer to a yes.

Here we are, a decade later. One of my favorite quotes from Coach Monty Williams says, "Everything is on the other side of hard."

The questions we have to answer are, "Am I willing to adapt? Am I willing to pivot? Am I willing to keep pushing, keep changing, and keep showing up, even though I'm not getting what I want right now, at this moment?" That answer can't be delivered through lip service. Your actions have to reflect the posture of relentless determination and grit.

Let me be clear: this is not a teaching on hustling. I am careful not to use that word, because I believe we're hustling ourselves to death. "Hustling" has sabotaged our overall wellness in ways Covid never could. Grit is a mindset, not a measure of hours contributed.

Grit is extreme ownership of our passion and purpose, and it's a skill that anyone can gain through determination and perseverance.

BOUNCING BACK WITH GRIT AND RESILIENCE

Angela Duckworth, author of *Grit* says:

> Grit is passion and perseverance for long-term goals.
> One way to think about grit is to consider what grit isn't.

Grit isn't talent. Grit isn't luck. Grit isn't how intensely, for the moment, you want something.

Instead, grit is about having what some researchers call an "ultimate concern"—a goal you care about so much that it organizes and gives meaning to almost everything you do. And grit is holding steadfast to that goal. Even when you fall down. Even when you screw up. Even when progress toward that goal is halting or slow.

Talent and luck matter to success. But talent and luck are no guarantee of grit. And in the very long run, I think grit may matter at least as much, if not more.

When I had my third stroke, I felt utterly leveled at first. My summer was going to be spent indoors, mostly alone. It was depressing! I have vivid memories of incredible frustration as I fought with insurance while trying to manage my rehabilitation. I can remember when I went to make food for myself, my hands barely working, and I can still feel the sorrow and pain that I experienced when I realized that I couldn't even open a jar on my own at that point in my recovery. My mom had a stroke around the same time, so I couldn't turn to her for words of wisdom and her guiding light as she had to focus all of her energy on her own recovery to keep her strength up.

I struggled and battled through that season by telling myself: *You are here for a purpose. Don't forget that. Just get through today. What's the 1 percent progress I can make today? Keep pushing. You'll get there.*

And eventually, I did.

Another example of grit happened when I was running a healthcare company. At 7 p.m. the night before a presentation (and just three weeks into my role as president), the owner came in my office and said, "I hear you have a big presentation to a new client we are trying to get. Are you ready for it?" Of course, I was, so I said "yes." His response? "Great, because I have a whole boardroom of people waiting to hear it so you can practice before the big show tomorrow." Most would have panicked and ran. But I am not one to back down from an opportunity no matter how scary it may be or how nervous I may be. I saw this as an opportunity to learn, to get better and thrive.

So at 7 p.m., I walked into that boardroom full of very seasoned executives waiting to hear my pitch. After less than 10 minutes of speaking, I was stopped and asked to start over so I could say my introduction with more conviction and heart. As I stayed in that boardroom until midnight practicing with the whole group over and over again until it was great, I learned something that truly set me up for success in life. I learned that it's in those defining moments, those moments where you are scared and tired and feel like you can't do any more, but you still dig in and keep going, that's when you develop an incredible amount of grit.

• • •

My grit was also tested during Covid—as I'm sure it was for many of you reading this book.

We've all got a story about how Covid affected our lives, families, and businesses. I'm no different. After being in private practice for 12 years as a mental skills coach, I had a solid client list at the beginning of 2020. Then overnight almost, one by one, many of my paying clients started dropping.

I understood. Money stopped rolling in. People had to tighten their financial belts in meaningful ways. Companies were shutting their doors in droves. By the spring of 2020, I had one paying client.

I was thankful that because I have a financial mentor on my personal board of directors, I had margin to pay the bills. But paying company bills wasn't the only challenge I faced. Like many of you, I had plenty of pent-up energy and passion that sent me around and around in mental circles. My Why Power is so big and pressing that if I'm not doing purposeful work, I'm restless. So what did I do?

I started working for free. I woke up every single morning and filmed a coaching video to post on Facebook. I thought *People are hurting. People need these mental tools now more than ever.* I knew this work was too important to wait for a new opportunity to present itself idly. So I started giving it away. But like anything in life, if you put good out, it comes back and in no time I was busier than ever.

Fast-forward a year and a half into quarantine and while things were much better, I hit a wall when a contract that was supposed to happen didn't actually happen. This was a hard hit for me, so I called a friend who just so happened to be sitting with Mark Cuban's producers at the very moment. "Have you heard of 'Fireside Chat'?" she asked.

I hadn't. "Fireside Chat" is a Cuban-backed podcasting app for content creators. I'd never done anything like it before. Still, I knew a pivot would be necessary for creating a greater impact for good and reaching more lives.

"Can you fly out to LA tomorrow?" she asked. Of course, my answer was yes and today, I'm on the show every morning at 10 a.m. I've got more business and work than I've ever had. But honestly, that's not even the point. The point is that I'm reaching and helping more people than I ever would have had it not been for the adversity ushered in by Covid and an international lockdown and roadblocks. It is in those movements that our grit is built and tested.

For most of us 2020 was the year of grit and adaptability. It changed schools, businesses, sports, interpersonal dynamics—you name it. Everyone had to adapt to a new way of life and fight through unexpected hardships. All the projections for 2020 went out the window, and everyone needed to come to terms with the new normal: online sales, Zoom calls, masks, virtual learning, stadiums with no fans, unknowns, and so much more.

This kind of adaptability is crucial for leadership because rarely do things go according to plan, and your job is to find fulfillment and purpose no matter what happens. If you are stubborn and set in your ways and refuse to pivot, then you will limit yourself (and your team) severely.

As an occupational therapist, I have trained for years to help people whose lives have not gone according to plan. I worked with a lot of people at all levels to find a new normal. I even worked with veterans to re-enter civilian life after combat.

I met a woman named Tianna who gave me permission to share her story. It's so powerful—such an accurate picture of grit—that I'm going to share it in her own words:

> I'm from a small town in Ohio. I knew my parents weren't going to pay for me to go to college, so I had to find my own way out. It was a classic if-you-don't-get-out-now-you'll-never-leave story. I worked really hard

and got both an academic and athletic scholarship to be a track and field long-jumper and sprint runner at the University of Tennessee (UT).

I wasn't necessarily an elite athlete at the time, but my father and I were really intentional in how I trained and the adjustments I was making every day to improve my game. When I got to Tennessee, I had a very normal freshman year—I got my butt kicked on a regular basis. But I did qualify for nationals. Then at nationals that year, I choked. I completely choked. The irony is that the week following nationals, I actually had one of the best races of my career. It was a performance breakthrough.

The worst had already happened (at nationals) and it was no longer something I was afraid of. In fact, if I'd ran the same race at nationals as I did the week after, I would have placed second as a freshman, which is kind of unheard of.

My sophomore year I was undefeated. I made team USA *and* I won the world championship. I thought, *OK. The season of adversity is behind me.* I was wrong. I signed a professional contract with Nike, which turned out to cause significant problems at UT, an Adidas-sponsored school. The university didn't want me to train on campus or even use their weight room. I had to wear clothes without labels, and even then, they made it incredibly difficult for me to get in training time.

Eventually I had to leave the school altogether. I moved to LA to train with Bobby Kersee and Jackie Joyner-Kersee. It felt like a dream. But those dreams were short-lived. For the next seven years, I proceeded to win exactly zero events. I couldn't outperform my college scores. I was stuck.

Seven years. 2,555 days marked by defeat. I struggled with depression, with suicidal thoughts and ideations, and I was diagnosed with chronic depression. I was embarrassed. My identity had been so rooted in being an elite athlete—a title I no longer felt the right to label myself with. I gave up long-jumping, but I continued to travel overseas to compete because I needed to pay bills and that was one way I could still earn a paycheck.

In my twenties, I found myself married to an abusive partner and at odds with my parents. At the same time, my game was slowly improving. I had my second performance breakthrough. Somehow, I made the Olympic Team in 2012 and even made it to the podium in the 4 × 100–meter relay, which earned me my first gold medal and world record.

And that's when the cognitive dissonance started— of being this total badass during the day and becoming a battered wife at night. It did a number on my psyche and it felt easier for me to just end my life. I had no control over anything—not even what I ate or what I wore. I thought winning would make the sacrifices I was making worth it. But it didn't.

No amount of gold could account for the brokenness I endured as a result of the abuse and narcissism of my partner. I was just about to hang myself on my own equipment in my garage gym when I was interrupted. Then there were two other occasions when I stopped in front of a train while living in Europe. Obviously, none of my suicidal ideations became a reality, but that isn't because I didn't crave it. I did.

When we imagine the worst-case scenarios, it's never what "worst-case" would actually be. Worst-case would be not making it through at all. The worst-case would be loss of life. Because as long as there's life, there's potential.

Tianna would leave her abusive partner, enter a new relationship, and give birth to her first child—a boy, born via emergency C-section just weeks after competing in the Olympic trials of 2021. That woman has more grit in her pinkie than most of us will experience in a lifetime. When I asked Tianna how she managed to keep going, year after year, setback after setback, how she kept bouncing back to compete another day, here's what she said: "I just started to give myself credit for surviving. I think a lot of us don't do that. We get so caught up in the fact that things are hard. We don't give ourselves credit for being 100 percent successful at getting through it. We're still back there, beating ourselves up for it being difficult at all."

If no one has told you lately that they're proud of you for surviving, I am. You should be proud of yourself for surviving, adapting, pivoting, and demonstrating grit during the chaos and uncertainty of 2020—because everyone needed grit that year. (See Figure 8.1.)

FIGURE 8.1. Strengthening your grit muscles requires you to practice on a daily basis—this graphic includes various concepts and goals that you can cultivate on an ongoing basis to strengthen your perseverance and passion.

HOW TO DEVELOP GRIT

So how do we develop grit? How do we "seek out suffering," as David Goggin suggests? On the surface, pursuing pain sounds a bit masochistic, right? It sounds barbaric. But think about it: We choose pain whenever we physically work out our bodies. We choose to sweat, be out of breath, and feel sore. We choose to suffer. Why can't the same be true for us when moving from grit to greatness?

According to the grit expert Angela Duckworth, there are four things we'll need to develop our grit muscle.

1. Practice

Much like the other disciplines we've studied together, grit is an art to be practiced. You might try and fail before you find success.

In 2002, entrepreneur Elon Musk formed Space Exploration Technologies Corporation, or SpaceX, in hopes of revolutionizing the aerospace industry. Musk knew the key to running a fiscally successful space shuttle program of his own would be creating a reusable rocket. Musk and his team worked tirelessly to construct a rocket that could theoretically launch, land vertically, and then be relaunched repeatedly.

Their first attempt failed.

Their second attempt failed.

Their third attempt failed.

Their fourth attempt failed.

But finally, on April 8, 2016, SpaceX launched and safely landed its first rocket.

The team behind this successful launch learned to reframe each "failure" as just another practice run to prepare for greatness. Each failure led to new information and provided data for what adjustments should be made for the next run.

Where can you launch your reusable rocket? Do you have an idea for a new business? Do you have a strategic innovation you've been dying to try? Show grit. Launch. If the rocket doesn't land, record what went wrong, make the necessary adjustments, and try again.

2. Purpose

We spent an entire chapter discussing the power of purpose. We need to find our Why and keep it front and center. Grit is impossible to demonstrate without it.

My mom went to work in pain, but she knew her purpose. She knew she had a family to take care of. And you know what? Sometimes putting food on the table is a good reason. It's an honorable reason. Without her level of grit, we may not have had shoes on our feet or beds to sleep in. Not all Whys have to be high-level career achievements. Your reason for this season could be that someone's got to keep the lights on. There is no shame in that. If you're still journeying toward finding your more significant purpose for existing on this planet, find a way to create a Why for today.

3. Hope

Hope comes as a result of purpose. I like to believe the word *hope* stands for "hold on, pain ends." Hope will pick you up off the floor and bring you back to purpose when you're tempted to quit or give up. Another way of saying this is to have *belief*. Believe that you have something unique to offer the world that no one else can. It's the truth, so embrace it.

My mentor and coach Jesse Itzler completed an Ultraman competition a few weeks ago. An Ultraman is a three-day triathlon with a 6.2-mile swim and 90-mile bike ride on day one, a 141.4-mile bike ride on day two, and a double marathon on day three. When asked how he trained, Jesse said he trained for two weeks in the cold waters of Lake Minnesota.

When asked, "Why did you do that to yourself?," he said it was his big yearly goal of accomplishing something that would push him beyond what he thought could be. He said *he wanted to be part of an elite group of people, "a club" that couldn't buy their way in, but had to earn it.*

I've never heard a grittier line in all my days of coaching!

It's worth mentioning that Jesse is in his fifties. He had *enough* self-belief, mental resiliency, and grit to finish it—and he did. He earned it.

4. Time

One of the main variables in the equation of grit is time. We want to succeed, and we want to succeed *today*. We're wired to be results-oriented, but instant gratification contradicts the nature of grit. We have to dig deep and settle in for the long haul, knowing that relentless determination produces greatness that endures.

After that third stroke, I had to do rehab daily to complete the most basic functions. For someone who likes to be on the move and enact change, having to live the same life every day doing things I "should" have been able to do is damn-near infuriating. I struggled and battled through that season by telling myself: *You are here for a purpose. Don't forget that. Just get through today. What's 1 percent progress I can make today? Keep pushing. You'll get there.* And eventually, I did. It took a lot of grit.

Exercise: Build Endurance

An active and introspective exercise for grit is constantly taking mental inventory as you work toward your goals. As you are working on a project, take note of the moments you can feel yourself checking out. When you're ready to throw in the towel on a meeting, task, or personal activity, ask yourself: Can I put in *just a little more*?

Maybe it's five more minutes; maybe it's much longer—the goal is to build your endurance and raise your threshold for persevering through things that you find difficult or mundane. The power to strive toward your end goal in the face of adversity is what grit is all about, and building your daily endurance sets you up for success when the big roadblocks come your way!

Grit isn't a shortcut.
It's a long way home.
You can't buy grit.
It's earned through quiet discipline.

TURNING THE PAGE

It's always been my philosophy: Turn the page. If something falls through, turn the page. It's over with, get used to it, and get on with it. Very simple. It's always worked for me.

—Merv Griffin,
American television show host and media mogul

We're in the home stretch. This final principle is essential to bounce back from a setback and, more important, move forward from a setback. It's time to turn the page.

I am fortunate to work with some of the highest-caliber people in professional sports and at the executive level. Most of my clients come to me with some of the skills we have unpacked in this book. The one skill that almost everyone I meet could make stronger is this one. I'm talking about the ability to turn the page on our own failures, shortcomings, mistakes, and disappointments.

FALLING SHORT

As a Lululemon ambassador, I'd spoken on their behalf many times and I was incredibly excited for the opportunity to speak as the closing keynote at one of their big, pop-up experiential events. During the event, things took longer than usual, and we were behind schedule. An assistant approached me and said, "Dar, we're going to have to cut your time down." She came back to me multiple times to say the same thing, and by the time I got onstage, I had to cut my talk in half.

Needless to say, before I even said my first word, I was worried. It turns out I had a reason to be. The talk didn't go well. It just felt off, and I was not in flow. It didn't hit the mark and everyone, including me, knew it. I never landed the plane—I never got my ultimate message across—which is the whole point of any talk.

This had never happened before, and I was so upset with myself and I wondered afterward, *How do I make this up? Can I send a video to everyone?*

I voiced my concerns to the event organizers and their response was simple: "Dar, it's done. It's not a big deal."

But it was a big deal to me. I couldn't get over it. I tortured myself for months about this speaking engagement, because every speech I give matters. Finally, it got to the point where I was tired of thinking about it and tired of losing sleep over it. I needed to do something to stop this event from disturbing my peace and ruling my thoughts.

I needed to learn from it and turn the page.

TURNING THE PAGE—EVEN WHEN IT'S DIFFICULT

As I've been writing this book, I've started experiencing bouts of headaches. Not occasionally, either. Almost daily. I decided to get an appointment with a neurologist because I wasn't sure if these headaches meant I was about to have that spectacular fourth stroke I'd been promised. Since it's been a while since I've seen a neurologist, I had to find a new one.

After filling in the doctor on my past strokes and their challenges, he said, "So, Dar, did I hear you say that you couldn't have kids?"

"Yes. Because I can't," I told him. I pointed to the spot over my head where the blood clot sat. "Remember?"

His face fell. He looked to the other doctor who consulted with him on my case. "Oh, Dar. Did someone tell you this should keep you from having children?"

"Yes," I said with a confused face.

"I'm so sorry," the doctor said, "but this blood clot shouldn't have stopped you from conceiving. There are many ways we could have made it safe for you to carry a child. Whoever told you that was wrong."

A flash of white-hot rage and gut-wrenching pain went through my entire body. I had no words at that moment—or in this one, honestly—to express how deeply emotional this revelation was to me. I lost so much when I embraced the idea that I'd never carry a baby. My marriage ended, and I've actively avoided relationships with men I knew wanted kids. I didn't want to put either of us through the process of having to choose between me and the traditional means of having a family. I created a vision of my life without a baby ever being a part of it and learned to get used to the idea after many years.

But now, everything I had lost because of an incorrect diagnosis flooded every part of me. I thought I was protecting my life and a potential baby's life, but that was wrong. Suddenly, a vision of a baby babbling, toddler giggles, kissing boo-boos, and coaching kids' little league swept over me.

If I hadn't done my work during my career, that news might have been enough to bury me for a while. And while I felt the massive weight of this news, I knew I needed to feel it but not get stuck in it, so before I could turn the page on this, I had to mentally make sense of it. So I turned to so many of the tools in my toolkit. I reframed it. I focused on all I was able to do with the time versus the time I lost. I revisited my mission and gifts. And I took the time to watch my game film from the last 26 years.

If I had had a child, I wouldn't have been able to use my gifts to live out my purpose at the same level. I wouldn't have been able to travel as much as I have and give the amount of time I do to my clients. I've reached more lives and helped more people around the world because I haven't had a family waiting for me back home. I feel like I have lots of young adult kids and brothers and sisters that I feel very blessed to call my family; they all just happen to be six foot six and in professional sports.

While I wish I had *known*—that's undeniable—I may have made the same choice, and the outcome might still be the same.

But I can't live in the what-ifs of missed opportunities, and neither can you. A car's rearview mirror is so small, and its windshield is so big because our lives are meant to be lived facing forward. Sometimes, there's no beautiful resolution or guarantee that things couldn't have gone a better way. That's uncomfortable for us, but it's also a reality beyond our control. Sometimes you must have faith that life, while at times unfair, is nothing less than a combination of what it's meant to be and what you've created it to be.

So I turned the page.

And you can, too.

Go ahead and turn the page.

Turn the page on the things and people that are toxic around you.

Turn the page on the unhealthy lifestyle that isn't serving you.

Turn the page on your relationship ending.

Turn the page on the meeting that flopped.

Turn the page on the proposal that was rejected.

Turn the page on the bad game.

Turn the page on the bad *year*.

And then think about what you are turning your page *to*.

Turn the page *to* your greatness.

Turn the page *to* your championship year.

Turn the page *to* bounce back.

Turn the page *to* new opportunities.

Turn the page *to* new people in your life.

Journal Prompts for Reflection

If you're struggling with processing these feelings and hardships, try journaling through them using these prompts:

1. What is this hardship?
   - Use the exercise "Micro to Macro" in Principle 7: Reframing Setbacks!
2. What did I learn from this?
3. What's the next step?
4. Now, turn the page.

Then follow through! Think of it like driving a car: this check-in is our glance in the rearview mirror to get our bearings before we settle our gaze back on the horizon and hit the gas to zoom forward on our journey.

TURNING THE PEOPLE PAGE

While all these examples deal with specific situations or scenarios, some of the most challenging scenarios to turn the page on are people.

I have allowed narcissists into my life who hurt, betrayed, and made me feel small. I've had people take advantage of me. I've had people use me. I've had people mistake my kindness for weakness. I had to turn the page on all of them.

There are some people who have been out of my life for years, and yet I still find myself wondering, *Why did I let that person in? Why did I trust him? Why did I share this part of my life with them?*

When you find yourself ruminating like this, it's time to say out loud, "OK, I'm turning the page."

It's OK to take a risk in a relationship or a business partner. It's OK to take a chance on friendship. It's OK to gamble on love. Even if something in your life didn't work out the way you thought it would, and maybe we should have seen it coming, it's OK that it happened.

But once you see people clearly, there's nothing left to do but to grow in wisdom and turn the page.

In Matthew McConaughey's book *Greenlights,* he recounts a story from his friend and former University of Texas football coach, the late Darrell Royal. Coach Royal had been a leader to many, including a musician McConaughey called Larry. Larry had hit it big—with several number one songs on the country music charts. He was seeing more fame and influence than he thought possible! The downside of all the new money and attention was that Larry had lost sight of his mission and picked up a drug habit on his journey to becoming a top performer.

At this time, Larry ran into Coach Royal (his mentor) at a party. He approached Coach Royal like he would have anytime before and told him a story. At the end of the story Coach Royal rested a hand on his shoulder, looked him in the eyes, and said something that would help him change the direction of his life.

"Larry," he said, "you got something on your nose there, bud."

McConaughey tells his reader that Larry was deeply ashamed to have let his mentor down that night. The next day he went over to Coach Royal's house and he apologized, expressing how he'd lost his way on the road to fame and would never intentionally disrespect the guidance the coach had offered him for all those years.

"What should I do?" he asked his coach.

"Larry," Coach Royal responded, "I have never had any trouble turning the page in the book of my life."

So Larry turned the page.

He didn't dwell on the past, replaying all the wrong decisions that got him there and wishing he could change them. No, he got the needed help, did the work, and recovered. He continues to work daily to maintain sobriety and be the best he can be, the man his coach knew he was meant to become.

Whatever adversity you're facing, whatever challenges you're steeped in, it's time for you to stop reading from that same script and instead simply turn the page.

COMMON DENOMINATORS

Years ago, I had a client who was an executive for a large corporation. She was one of those people who just likes to be mad. If I'd had let her, every one of our sessions would have revolved around her, complaining and venting about the ineffective and old-school ways the board was run. But it wasn't just the board who was at fault for the adversity she was facing. It was also her ex-husband, her former employer, a friend, and a nosy neighbor. According to my client, "everyone" conspired to make her unhappy and unsuccessful.

"You'll never *believe* what so-and-so said."

"So-and-so is at it again."

"If it weren't for so-and-so, we could actually get things done."

And when I'd ask her, "So, what's your role? What part of this breakdown can you own?" she'd shrug and move along. She wouldn't even pretend to consider that maybe, *just maybe*, she'd served some role in the newest conflict.

After meeting with this client for a while, I got out a sheet of paper. I said, "How are you at math?" She told me she was decent. I wrote down a series of fractions:

1/4, 3/4, 13/4, 37/4

I said, "What do you notice about these fractions?"

"They all have four as a common denominator."

"If I listed out all the situations you're frustrated about right now, what one person would they have in common?"

"Me."

Bingo.

If your life or career is filled with conflict and frustration, it's time to look in the mirror. Be honest with yourself. Stop blaming other people—or even life itself—for situations you are contributing to or downright causing. I know you are a good person. I do. But we've got very little time left together in this book, so I can't go easy on you.

My client didn't get "unstuck" in that one session. It took several months of meeting weekly for her to retract that finger she had become so set on pointing at others for what I'm guessing was her entire career to date. But slowly, through watching her own game film and practicing EQ, she was able to start identifying her role in the problem.

If you feel stuck right now, I want you to make a list of all the reasons you feel stuck. What people, obstacles, and circumstances are keeping you from bouncing back? Take a look at your list. What's the common denominator to everything you wrote down?

You.

Listen, I'm not saying you're the problem. But if we can train our brains to seek out our part in any given conflict, it will only help us grow. It will help us turn the page on whatever issue you're facing much faster so we can bounce back better than before.

Let me give you a little bit of an extreme example. I've been having some trouble with my shoulder freezing up on me. So I went to the doctor to get a cortisone shot—something I'd never done before. I sat down, got the shot, and went to move my shoulder to see if I could yet feel the effects of the steroids. Not only could I *not* move my shoulder, but I couldn't move my entire arm.

"Just give it a minute," the doctor said.

A week later, my arm still wasn't right. I had no mobility in my entire arm or hand. After some physical therapy, the feeling started coming back, but it's slow progress. Throughout this experience, it was tempting to place blame. To immediately go to, "That doctor screwed up my arm." And you know what? Maybe he did have a part in where he placed the needle, or how strong the dosage was, or whatever. It's also been tempting to say: "How could this happen to me? How did I get *another* injury at a doctor's office? What are the odds? Why do these terrible things keep happening to me? How can I write a book if I can't use one hand?"

But that line of thinking gets me nowhere. It's an unreasonable concept. One of the main problems with blame is that it's based on an expectation of fairness. I don't have to tell you this, but life isn't fair. It wasn't fair yesterday, and it won't be fair tomorrow. Life isn't more or less fair for anyone.

So stop blaming and start owning.

The turn-the-page mentality tells me that the first thing I need to do in any situation where I'm hurt or frustrated is to ask, "What is my part?" The turn-the-page mentality prompts you to watch your game film of any given experience and critique your performance. Once your reaction to hurt or anger or disappointment or betrayal becomes, "What could I have done differently?" I'm telling you, the grip that situation has on you will begin to loosen, followed by acceptance, and soon enough, you'll be bouncing back stronger than ever before.

So what did turning the page practically look like after that cortisone shot? It looked like getting back to work. In fact, I had to leave the doctor's office and head straight to a coaching session. There wasn't anything they could do for me in that moment and I sure as heck wasn't going to let something like a faulty arm derail my day and delay my mission.

On the drive over, I thought, *If this becomes permanent and I can't use this arm, it's OK, I'll use my right arm anyhow. I could get a program to help me write. I'll find some options to build muscle in the gym. I'll make a plan.*

It was the same when I had my third stroke. I thought to myself, *if something happens and I lose some function, I'll just devise a plan to compensate for it. Right now, I have to turn the page. I have to move on.*

Today, I've trained my brain to immediately reframe adversity, so it doesn't keep me from bouncing back. It took years, but I'm finally there—and I share that because the same can be true for you. You've read over 150 pages of content now that gives you the tools to bounce back in any—and I mean any situation. So what's stopping you?

You know you're the only thing that can hold you back. So get moving and turn the page.

PUTTING IT ALL TOGETHER AND INTO PRACTICE

*Celebrate what you've accomplished, but raise
the bar a little higher each time you succeed.*

**—Mia Hamm,
American retired professional soccer player,
two-time Olympic gold medalist, and two-time
FIFA Women's World Cup champion**

MY HOPE FOR YOU

When I began writing this book, the art of bouncing back was supposed to be a *chapter*, not a *whole book*. I started to put together the game plan of the principles that helped me and my clients bounce back, and it quickly became far more than a chapter. It became an entire game plan, and *this* is the exact game plan. You are getting it all. I want you to not only read this but *apply it*. Absorb all of the information that you've read in these pages, apply the work you've put into the exercises in each chapter, and then move it into your heart. Feel these changes and then put them into your hands and do something about it! Bounce back faster, so that you can reach your greatness. I truly believe that every single person on this planet has greatness to achieve and a unique mission powered by their gifts, which the *world* deserves to see.

Don't get overwhelmed. Just get going on putting the principles into practice.

Let's go over the highlight reel one more time together.

BOUNCE BACK PRINCIPLE 1:
EMBRACE THE SUCK

We're realists, right? That means we know life is going to keep on throwing us curveballs. Sometimes we'll hit them out of the park, but most times curveballs will throw us for a loop. Whether you're facing a traumatic injury, a job loss, the passing of a loved one, a relationship that's falling apart, or a perspective-shifting experience that makes you question your faith; things are going to happen that rock you to your core and challenge your commitment to your life's purpose. Embrace the suck while it's happening because you're prepared to move through it. Remember, you control no situation, but you do control your reaction to the unexpected. You have a choice between lingering in the lows of life or facing these challenges head-on with a mental toolkit that you've cultivated for comebacks. It's important to remember that your setbacks don't define you and that every comeback you make continues to refine you, strengthening your grit muscles and allowing you to stand even firmer in your life's mission.

BOUNCE BACK TAKEAWAY

Embrace the suck. Use it.
Learn from it. Rise from it. Repeat.

BOUNCE BACK PRINCIPLE 2: UNDERSTAND WHO YOU ARE

Who are you? What are your gifts, skills, and talents? How do you work and communicate best? You know all of that now and at the end of the day, understanding *who you are* is vital when trying to achieve things you've never done before or to bounce back from whatever is holding you down. By taking the time to *discover* your Fundamental Hardwiring, you were able to identify and communicate your gifts, talents, and skill sets that will help keep you in your personal flow state going forward.

Coming out of the major setback of the pandemic, it has never been more relevant to understand exactly who you are and what drives your purpose. Take the time to practice Active Awareness when it comes to identifying your Fundamental Hardwiring, who fuels it to bring out the best in you, and who triggers it to create stress and anxiety. Keep your focus on staying in flow by identifying the people, environments, and activities that support your best flow state. When setbacks happen, you will bounce back quicker when you rely on yourself, your gifts, and your purpose. You are amazing, just saying it in case you forgot!

BOUNCE BACK TAKEAWAY

You are amazing, unique, and powerful.
Stay aligned and focused on this.

BOUNCE BACK PRINCIPLE 3: SEEK AND APPLY FEEDBACK

When it comes to bouncing back, it's very important to disconnect from your ego and seek feedback. Sometimes that's through watching film of yourself by replaying situations in your mind with an analytical lens. For athletes, it's quite literal: they watch recordings of themselves playing. For the rest of us, we need to get a little creative: record your meetings, live talks, or creative process. Whether you're observing yourself in flow or you're observing yourself stumbling, take note. What can you improve? What did you handle with grace and efficiency?

Most times, watching film of yourself isn't enough. You'll need the support of others. Are there things that they notice that you never thought of? Are they confirming what you know to be true? Use this to remind yourself what you're capable of!

When it's not confidence that you need, but a grounding presence to check you out of your ego, don't fear feedback. We've got to mentally train ourselves to evaluate ourselves and really hear the evaluations of others. If our own actions are keeping us in setback mode, we need outside parties to come in and provide the clarity we need to bounce back. Seek out feedback (from others and by rewatching your film) with an open mind because it strengthens and refines us in ways nothing else can.

> ## BOUNCE BACK TAKEAWAY
>
> **Don't be afraid to ask others for feedback and really listen.**

BOUNCE BACK PRINCIPLE 4: DISCOVER YOUR WHY POWER

If you were stranded on a desert island with only three things, you would want water, a pair of comfortable shoes, and your Why Power to get off that island. While water and shoes will be necessary for survival, it's your Why Power that will get you off that island. Remember, you first need to have a clear Mission Statement and Power Word to boil down your Why Power into a potent revival tonic. Your Mission Statement keeps you aligned with the things that matter most in your life. Your Power Word a quick jolt of inspiration whenever you need a reminder of why you're doing what you're doing.

With a strong commitment to your Why Power, setbacks feel more like a bump in the road rather than a dead end. Because of the work you've done, you will be able to bounce back and level up better than ever because you know there is something bigger than your ego driving you.

I wrote this book to follow my mission: *Inspire, empower, and awaken greatness in myself and others globally.* My bumper sticker for the world to see is *greatness.* What's yours?

BOUNCE BACK TAKEAWAY

Your Why Power is what sets you apart.

BOUNCE BACK PRINCIPLE 5: CREATE YOUR BOUNCE BACK ENVIRONMENT

Take a look around you right now. Where are you? What does your space look like? Who are you surrounding yourself with? Your mindset is 100 percent impacted by your various environments, physical, mental, social, sensory, and so on. The more in control you are of your environments, the easier it will be to come back from setbacks and push past limiting beliefs and plateaus.

Mental clutter and chaos are a part of everyone's life, but training yourself to be conscious of the environments you step into will keep the mess in your head at bay. Creating an environment that supports your Fundamental Hardwiring is crucial to finding your flow and setting you up to raise the bar in your life. The power of your senses and the influence of the people around you plays a crucial role in your success, so be sure to create an environment that helps you thrive.

BOUNCE BACK TAKEAWAY

It's all about environment, environment, environment.

BOUNCE BACK PRINCIPLE 6: ACTIVATE EMOTIONAL INTELLIGENCE

It's easy to take credit for our wins in life but owning up to our actions when we're not at our best . . . not so much. That's where Agility, Neutrality, and Accountability come in. These three words should be the building blocks for strengthening your Emotional Intelligence (EQ), which helps you to push through in times of stress, trauma, and setback. We all know that we can emotionally react to a situation, lose our cool, be too sensitive, or waffle back and forth on our feelings. Our ability to regulate our emotions and respond to the emotions of others—while also taking responsibility for both—is critical for getting out of the bad and making the most of the good in life.

We need to debunk the myth that being in touch with our emotions makes us weaker. It's time to raise up the truth: allowing yourself to manage the inventory of your emotional state is the pathway to more productive and positive interactions with the people around you. And these three tools are what you need to do exactly that:

1. **Emotional Agility:** Remain ever flexible. Bend to the storms passing through your life at the moment, but never break.
2. **Emotional Neutrality:** Sometimes a situation or setback will send us into fight-or-flight mode, but being emotionally intelligent in these situations looks like taking a level-headed approach. Emotional Neutrality allows you to stop the freak-out and put time and distance between you and the bad situation so you can intelligently respond in a healthy and productive way.
3. **Emotional Accountability:** EQ doesn't require perfection, but it does require you take responsibility for those times when your emotions get the best of you. Being accountable builds trust in our most important relationships.

BOUNCE BACK TAKEAWAY

Be responsible for your greatness and your opportunities by using the three building blocks of EQ: Emotional Agility, Neutrality, and Accountability.

BOUNCE BACK PRINCIPLE 7: REFRAME SETBACKS

It's not about being an eternal optimist. It's about perspective. Reframing is one of the coolest tools in your mental toolkit when it comes to making the terrible days bearable and the bad days much easier. The reality is there's almost always more than one way to look at any given situation. Understanding how to train our minds to reframe adversity as opportunity is how we begin to reframe the game. How you look at a situation has a massive impact on the decisions we make day in and day out. Zoom out from the difficult situations and always try to see the big picture. Is the adversity you're facing right now really a burned-down house with only ashes left, or is it a small house fire with a sturdy foundation remaining? Always ask yourself, what are all the ways that you can interpret a tough situation? How can adversity connect you to your purpose, help you push past limitations, or create an opportunity you never thought you'd have?

BOUNCE BACK TAKEAWAY

You can always recharge and revitalize by reframing.

BOUNCE BACK PRINCIPLE 8: CULTIVATE GRIT

We are so much stronger than we give ourselves credit for. Think of every challenge-filled setback you've experienced in your life. There have been a lot, right? Yet you're still here. You survived and honestly, are probably in a better position than you thought you'd be when the setback first happened.

We're only as weak as our mental fortitude permits us to be. Far too often, we stop just short of overcoming challenges and reaching our greatness because we haven't developed our grit muscle. Grit is about staying the course no matter how tired, anxious, afraid, or hopeless you think things are at the moment. It's about pushing through the hard stuff because you know you can handle it and you are committed to your Why Power. Having mental and emotional grit to adapt to any situation will build an unbeatable resiliency that helps us bounce back and persevere. Is the old adage, "When the going gets tough, the tough get going," ringing a bell here? Because it should!

Everyone has grit and it helps us prioritize our thoughts and strategies, informs our decisions, and gets us through the relentless pursuit of a singular goal or ideal.

We all develop grit through:

- **Practice:** You might try and fail before you find success—everyone does. Make adjustments and then try again.
- **Purpose:** Keeping what drives you at the forefront of your mind is vital to persevering through setbacks. Grit will keep you going longer.

- **Hope:** Remember this, "hold on, pain ends," or hope. Believe that you can get past whatever is hurting or haunting you and offer the world something unique that no one else can.
- **Time:** We have to dig deep and settle in for the long haul, knowing that relentless determination produces greatness that endures.

No matter what, just keep going.

BOUNCE BACK TAKEAWAY

You can do it, dig deep, and keep at it, again and again. Your grittiness will lead to greatness.

BOUNCE BACK TAKEAWAY 9:
TURN THE PAGE

Turning the page isn't easy, but honestly, what is? Sometimes, moving forward and letting what you cannot change go requires introspection that makes you uncomfortable. That's OK. Do the hard work. Make setbacks, traumas, conflicts, and all the rest of the bad stuff stay in the past once you pull through it. You don't need to keep the memory of your past issues in your current mindset. You lived through it and are a better person for it. It's time for a new story that highlights your greatness.

Here's how you do it. Ask yourself what people, obstacles, and circumstances are keeping you from bouncing back? Once you identify them, stop playing the blame game, and own your part in difficult situations. Turning the page asks you to look inward, own what you're responsible for, let go of what you cannot change, and move forward with the knowledge that you can approach a difficult situation differently next time if you need to! Release the past and focus on the positives of the future. Soon enough, you'll be bouncing back stronger than ever before.

BOUNCE BACK TAKEAWAY

Don't look back, instead turn the
page and bounce forward.

• • •

With those nine principles and the incredible hard work you've done to get to this point, I know you can bounce back from *any* setback. And I hope you know that, too.

GREATNESS COMES WITH CONSISTENCY

True story. About 48 hours before my editor's absolutely last possible extension on the manuscript for this book, I was sweating at the finish line. No joke. I didn't have an ending. I was out of writing extensions. And even though I believe every word in this book to be true, useful, and transformational, there are still times when the conversation in my head does a number on me. "Does this stuff really make a difference? Does it really matter to anyone, Dar?"

Well, an end-of-the-day conversation changed that conversation in my head almost instantly. While I was working with an NFL player who's been in the league over a decade, I asked him an off-the-cuff question, "What do you think it takes to win a Super Bowl?"

"Dar, it takes consistency and the ability to bounce back."

Uh, did he just reflect back to me what I've been writing? I was amazed.

I asked him to elaborate.

"You need to consistently get better each week. Making yourself and your team better than you were last week requires that you keep bringing it over and over with no letup." He said this like it was overly obvious to everyone. He kept on.

"And then, when everyone on the team keeps bringing it with consistency, it's the team that consistently bounces back from a loss, a bad play, or whatever comes their way. With consistency, the team becomes so mentally good and resilient at bouncing back from setbacks. When you pair those two, you'll see a championship team."

I was stunned. He, without prompting, echoed my coaching back to him. When a team becomes so mentally good and resilient at bouncing back from setbacks, they become champions. When he shared with me that consistency and bounce back were the elements needed to win the Super Bowl, I just smiled.

When you (and those in your life) take the principles from the Bounce Back System and apply them consistently, you will become more mentally resilient and bounce back faster each time life throws something at you. You have your own Super Bowls to win figuratively.

When you apply consistency to the principles in this book, you will rise higher like that bouncy ball hitting the wall harder. You will grow, and not just survive but thrive and win the championship of life!

MY GRATITUDE FOR YOU

I've been blessed to help people all over the world overcome the most extreme odds. In reading this book, hopefully you understand my passion for my mission and the extreme odds that I've personally had to overcome to continue pursuing it. When I ask people what they want to be remembered for, I almost always reference ESPN's *30 for 30* segment. They're one of my favorites because it's never about someone's life being a breeze. Instead, it's always someone who had to overcome seemingly insurmountable odds and bounced back even when everything was against them. As we show up for life, our *30 for 30* is in the making. If you apply these principles, you can bounce back and have one of the most epic stories that we will ever get to watch! A story that inspires anyone who hears it.

Life is not always easy as pie; we're always bouncing back from *something*. But you know what? *We are resilient.* The human spirit is resilient. It's a choice every day to get up, bounce back from our setbacks, and raise the bar in our lives as well as the lives of those around us.

Thanks to all of the time and effort you put into bouncing back, you're now prepared to confidently answer the question: "How are you going to show up?" Right now, you have a 100 percent bounce back rate. Every single thing in your life that has been hard for you so far, you overcame. And now you have tools to help you bounce back even faster every time.

If you're reading this paragraph, it's my hope that you absorbed all the principles and are now ready to start applying them right away! The only way your life will change is if you make a choice to change it. So let this be your choice. Let this be your sign. Let this be your motivation. Let me be the wind in your sails right now. Let this message give you the oxygen you need to keep going. Why? Because we need you. And we're going to do this together. Life is not meant to be done alone.

We're meant to do this together. Find people around you who can help, support, mentor, and guide you. Stay connected with me. I post inspiring content all the time on all my social platforms. You can find me at @TheCoachDar on Instagram, LinkedIn, or Twitter. You can also listen in on my daily show on Fireside called Awakening Greatness, at firesidechat.com/darleensantore. Shoot me a direct message or an email at CoachDar.com—tell me how you're bouncing back. I'll really hear you.

More important, if you've gotten to this point, I want to say *thank you*. Seriously, thank you for picking up this book. Thank you for being a part of my journey. Thank you for trusting me on this. Thank you for sharing it with the people in your lives; I hope that you can pay it forward to someone who is going through a hard time and needs some tools to bounce back. I've had three strokes, so being able to write is not only a blessing, but quite the challenge even with help along the way. This is my first book, but hopefully it won't be my last. I'll be doing my damnedest to keep raising the bar while sharing more of my knowledge and experience with you.

I want to leave you with a powerful message as you go into the world and start putting the Bounce Back System principles into practice. Scan the QR code for a video from me directly to you.

And, with that . . .

Let's get resilient.

Let's keep building our mental toolkit.

Let's keep bouncing back.

Let's go raise the bar!

To your greatness,

Coach Dar

ACKNOWLEDGMENTS

First and foremost, I want to thank Jesus for giving me the gift to be able to serve those around me. I wouldn't be here to tell this story if it wasn't for Him.

I want to thank my sister, Denise, and the rest of my family for always being there for me. And Dad, all those years of watching game film have finally paid off!

Thank you to Erik Olsson, who believed in me and took a chance on me when I came to him years ago with the idea for this book. I wouldn't have made it to the finish line if it wasn't for you, Erik. Thank you, my friend, for your mentorship, friendship, support, and guidance. I am forever grateful for you and Tricia.

Immense gratitude to Cheryl Segura, my amazing editor, and the entire team at McGraw Hill Publishing. Thank you for your trust and confidence in me and for supporting me every step of the way. Cheryl, you have a true gift with editing.

Thank you to my friend Jon Gordon for your mentorship, guidance, and friendship that you have provided me over the years. You and your work have made such an impact on my life.

Charlie Fusco and the entire team at TGC Worldwide have been extraordinary throughout this process. I wouldn't have been able to reach the finish line without your hard work, belief, dedication, commitment, and refinement.

Thank you to Esther Fedorkevich and the team at the Fedd Agency for believing in me and for this incredible opportunity. It has been incredible watching this book grow from concept to reality.

Kyle Negrete, I can't thank you enough for going to bat for me and for helping me to find an amazing publisher. Your prayers and guidance are much appreciated.

Shannon Jones, there are no words. . . . I definitely couldn't get to where I am today without your help on this book and everything we do within the business. You are my constant support, guardian, and friend.

Thank you to my dear friends Jessica and Jeff Reinhart, who have been there throughout this entire process. From the time this book was only a concept in my head, to whiteboarding all my ideas out at your house, you have been with me every step of the way.

Thanks also to Dr. Jason Kolber for all your support and the amazing introductions you made along the way.

Thanks to Holly Crawshaw for getting this process started and for all our amazing conversations. I am grateful for the time and effort that you put into this.

Thank you, Sara Schumacher, for always being available to lend a hand where needed.

To all my amazing clients, it has been a tremendous honor to work with each of you.

To all my friends who have supported me along the way (you know who you are), thank you from the bottom of my heart!

NOTES

PRINCIPLE 1

1. https://www.etonline.com/tiger-woods-undergoes-5th-back
-surgery-159264.

PRINCIPLE 2

1. https://www.amazon.com/Path-Creating-Your-Mission
-Statement-ebook/dp/B0042XA3B2.
2. https://www.helblingsearch.com/Blog-Item-Personality
-Testing-Proceed-with-Caution.
3. https://scottbarrykaufman.com/wp-content/uploads/2015
/02/Social-Psychological-and-Personality-Science-2014
-Sheldon-1948550614555028.pdf.

PRINCIPLE 3

1. Kobe Bryant, *The Mamba Mentality: How I Play*, MCD: 2018.
2. Bryant, 2018.
3. Flinders University, "Why People Become Defensive
and How to Address It: Addressing Why Defensiveness
Manifests Will Help Relationships, Conflict Management
and Decision Making to Reduce Defensiveness," *ScienceDaily*,
December 1, 2020, www.sciencedaily.com/releases/2020/12
/201201103610.htm.

PRINCIPLE 5

1. https://www.newportinstitute.com/programs/anxiety/.
2. https://journals.sagepub.com/doi/abs/10.1177/0146167209352864.
3. https://www.newportinstitute.com/resources/mental-health/executive-functioning-skills/.
4. https://www.newportinstitute.com/resources/mental-health/physical-environment-affect-you/.
5. Belknap Press, 2009.
6. University of Exeter, "Why Plants in the Office Make Us More Productive," *ScienceDaily*, September 1, 2014, www.sciencedaily.com/releases/2014/09/140901090735.htm.
7. American Chemical Society, "Particle Emissions from Laser Printers Might Pose Health Concern," *ScienceDaily*, August 2, 2007, www.sciencedaily.com/releases/2007/07/070731103629.htm.
8. https://greenbusinessbureau.com/green-practices/healthy-buildings/biophilia-and-biophilic-design-incorporating-sustainability-into-the-built-environment/.
9. S. Krauss Whitbourne, "5 Reasons Why Clutter Disrupts Mental Health," *Psychology Today*, May 13, 2017, https://www.psychologytoday.com/us/blog/fulfillment-any-age/201705/5-reasons-why-clutter-disrupts-mental-health.
10. https://www.psychologytoday.com/us/blog/fulfillment-any-age/201705/5-reasons-why-clutter-disrupts-mental-health.
11. Dennis Y. Hsu, et al., "The Music of Power: Perceptual and Behavioral Consequences of Powerful Music," *Social Psychological and Personality Science*, August 2014, DOI: 10.1177/1948550614542345.
12. https://www.verywellmind.com/why-do-we-associate-memories-so-strongly-with-specific-smells-5203963#:~:text=Scientists%20believe%20that%20smell%20and,very%20vivid%20when%20it%20happens.
13. https://www.verywellmind.com/why-do-we-associate-memories-so-strongly-with-specific-smells-5203963.

14. J. Y. Lee, H. Jun, S. Soma, et al., "Dopamine Facilitates Associative Memory Encoding in the Entorhinal Cortex," *Nature*, September 22, 2021, doi:10.1038/s41586-021-03948 -8.
15. https://spoonuniversity.com/lifestyle/studies-show-chewing -gum-could-actually-boost-your-memory#:~:text=The %20repetitive%20motion%20of%20chewing,concentrate %20and%20improves%20your%20memory.

PRINCIPLE 6
1. https://www.ihhp.com/meaning-of-emotional-intelligence/.

PRINCIPLE 7
1. https://www.ncbi.nlm.nih.gov/pmc/articles/PMC5767148.
2. L. Campbell-Sills, D. H. Barlow, T. A. Brown, and S. G. Hofmann, "Effects of Suppression and Acceptance on Emotional Responses of Individuals with Anxiety and Mood Disorders," *Behavioral Research and Therapy*, 2006; 44(9): 1251–1263, doi: 10.1016/j.brat.2005.10.001.
3. J. Meyer, *You Can Begin Again: No Matter What, It's Never Too Late*, FaithWords, 2015.
4. https://www.psychologytoday.com/us/blog/the-athletes-way /202103/4-reasons-writing-things-down-paper-still-reigns -supreme#:~:text=In%20addition%20to%20being%20faster ,areas%20and%20better%20memory%20recall.
5. Jon Gordon, "Jon Gordon Weekly Newsletter," March 30, 2015, https://jongordon.com/positive-tip-get-to.html.
6. https://www.forbes.com/sites/jodiecook/2021/02/22 /pressure-is-a-privilege/?sh=69b3d277de27.

INDEX

Page numbers followed by *f* refer to figures.

ABOUT THE AUTHOR

Darleen Santore, also known as "Coach Dar," is a licensed, board-certified occupational therapist; a globally sought-after motivational speaker; coach; executive; and the CEO and founder of the coaching firm Performance Meets Purpose Consulting. Known for her mental conditioning work with athletes in the NBA, NHL, MLB, MLS, and NFL, she has served as the mental skills coach for the Phoenix Suns. In addition to professional athletes, Coach Dar coaches and advises Fortune 100 executives, world leaders, artists, and entrepreneurs. Coach Dar's approach helps her clients dramatically improve their performance and purpose by helping them awaken to their greatness and to show up with a higher level of EQ and excellence.